MIGUEL DE CERVANTES SAAVEDRA was born in Spain in 1547 to a family once proud and influential but fallen on hard times. His father, a poor barber-surgeon, wandered up and down Spain in search of work. Educated as a child by the Jesuits in Seville, the creator of *Don Quixote* grew up to follow the career of a professional soldier. He was wounded at Lepanto in 1571, captured by the Turks in 1575, imprisoned for five years, and finally was rescued by the Trinitarian friars in 1580. On his return to Spain he found his family more impoverished than ever before. Supporting his mother, two sisters, and an illegitimate daughter, he settled down to a literary career and had hopes of becoming a successful playwright, but just then the youthful Lope de Vega entered triumphantly to transform the Spanish theater by his genius. *Galatea,* a pastoral romance, was published in 1585, the year of Cervantes' marriage to Catalina de Palacios y Salazar Vozmediano. But it did not bring him an escape from poverty, and he was forced to become a roving commissary for the Spanish armada. This venture, which led to bankruptcy and jail, lasted for fifteen years. Although he never knew prosperity, Cervantes did gain a measure of fame during his lifetime, and Don Quixote and Sancho Panza were known all over the world. Part I of *Don Quixote* was published in 1605; in 1613 his *Exemplary Novels* appeared, and these picaresque tales of romantic adventure gained immediate popularity. *Journey to Parnassus,* a satirical review of his fellow Spanish poets, appeared in 1614, and Part II *of Don Quixote* in 1615, as well as *Eight Plays and Eight Tragedies.* Miguel de Cervantes died in 1616, ten days before the death of Shakespeare—his English contemporary, his only peer.

INTERLUDES

Miguel de Cervantes

A New Translation and with a Foreword
BY EDWIN HONIG

Published by THE NEW AMERICAN LIBRARY
of CANADA LIMITED

CONTENTS

for Ramón Sender

FOREWORD

I   These eight short plays are among the most
beguiling things Cervantes ever wrote. Part of their
charm is the appropriateness of the simple dramatic form
to Cervantes' lighthearted, often elusive treatment of his
subjects. This is notable in a writer whose ingenuity in
creating character was offset by his casual use of literary
forms. Except for *The Siege of Numantia*, his plays read
like episodic narratives, his stories like dialogues and
dramatic sketches, and his best-known novel is a hodge-
podge of tall tales and long-winded colloquies from which
his main characters are often excluded. His pastoral
novels, *La Galatea* and *Persiles y Sigismunda*, written
according to anachronistic formulas, fail badly; his poetry
is often blank verse or a kind of rhymed prose. And
when he hastily completed Part II of *Don Quixote*, he
did so in self-protection because a literary opportunist
named Avellaneda, whom nobody has yet identified, had
had the gall to write and publish a fraudulent sequel to
the widely popular Part I.

So the formal and evidently deliberate achievement
of these dramatic pieces is something unusual in the
Cervantes canon. The interlude (*entremés*) is usually
dominated by its farcical tone. It is made up of a short
comic incident and is meant to be performed between the
acts of a full-length play in order to quiet an audience.
It deals with stock characters and a temporarily un-
hinged situation reassembled at the end by a token ban-
quet, dance, or marriage. In these respects little had

changed since the days of ancient Plautine comedy, on which were patterned the situations and character types of the *entremés*. But Cervantes' own account of his indebtedness turns blithely on the ironic distortions of personal experience. He remembers as a boy watching the actor-writer Lope de Rueda set up a crude stage in the town square and put on plays "with the greatest imaginable skill and sense of decorum" in front of "an old blanket drawn both ways by cords." What particular plays or how many of them Cervantes saw he does not say. Neither does he mention the earlier Spanish prototypes of the popular theater in the late Middle Ages, when performing troubadours (*juglares*) produced their farces on current subjects in the public squares. Nor does he mention two of his own contemporaries, Juan de Timoneda, who translated Plautus and wrote farces, or Juan de la Cueva, who imitated the classical dramatists and wrote interludes as well. The name of the greatest of his forerunners, Gil Vicente, the Portuguese-Spanish poet-dramatist, is likewise missing from his account. What needs to be added to his statement, then, is that through such sources, enriched by borrowings from the highly popular *commedia dell' arte*, Cervantes wrote the most distinguished pieces in a dramatic genre that has flourished in Spain for centuries under various names—*paso, auto, entremés, sainete, género chico*.

His interludes turn up in the collection *Eight Plays and Eight Interludes: New and Never Performed,* issued in 1615, the year before he died. How they came to be published Cervantes describes in the Prologue (see p. xxv). So we know that the by-then-famous author of *Don Quixote* saw them published by a bookseller eager to make the most he could of a new work by an established writer. Cervantes ruefully summarizes his vain attempts to return to the theater, which he had left in the 1580's:

. . . thinking the times were still the same as when they sang my praises, I again began to write a few plays. But I found no birds in last year's nests—I mean, I found no managers who wanted them, although they knew I had them. And so, I put them away in a trunk, consecrating and condemning them to eternal silence. In good time a bookseller told me he might buy them from me, although a royally licensed stage manager had told him that a good deal could be expected from my prose, but from my poetry, nothing at all. To tell the truth, I was certainly pained to hear this, and I said to myself, "Either I have changed and become another person or the times have improved immensely—which is generally the other way around, since people always praise the days gone by."

Always on the outside of literary society and lagging behind its fashions, Cervantes did not recoup the slight reputation he may have had as a dramatist thirty years earlier. But with the unexpected success of *Don Quixota*, and just turned sixty-five, he was embarked on a fresh literary career, producing novels, stories, and poems, as well as the book of plays.

The collection of *Eight Plays and Eight Interludes* belongs to this profoundly lighthearted period. Among the full-length plays are three takeoffs on his own traumatic experiences as a slave; a religious romance; one about a wandering actor among the Gypsies; and another about a thief turned holy man. (Yet the best-known of his plays, *The Siege of Numantia* [1585], a national epic of resistance in Roman times, was not included in the collection.) Posterity took his ironic subtitle literally: the plays are still almost "never performed." This is only relatively less true of the interludes, which are written in a condensed version of the episodic form characteristic of all his narratives. They concern the contemporary underworld and the middle- and lower-brow society of small towns and cities—country bumpkins, divorce courts, magicians, impostors, unemployed soldiers, unsheltered students, ineffectual husbands, saucy maids, irritable housewives, fatuous sacristans, garrulous whores. His most frequently revived, if not most intriguing, farce, *The Cave of Salamanca,* brings in the prevalent addiction to necromancy just when the action is about to descend into self-congratulatory adultery. The ingenious student who momentarily rescues middle-class respectability gets a tasty dinner for his trouble—a reward that almost equals the sum Cervantes got for his book of plays.

II   Always wanting to be a dramatist and a poet, Cervantes was destined to become the world's foremost novelist. Still, what he achieves in the interludes is something very close to the concentrative spirit of poetry and something characteristically dramatic as well. They might be called dramatic poems, as Ricardo Rojas has noted —and not merely because two of them are written in blank verse. They are brief, completely rounded-off, self-sufficient pieces, achieving a tightness of form that cannot be found in his work in the other genres. Their modesty of aim and slightness of incident are belied by the full-blooded particularity of their characters. For these are not stock types going through their paces in a well-worn anecdote, but vital individuals with distinct voices. They are dramatic in the way that Don Quixote and Sancho Panza are dramatic: their voices engage each other and depend on each other; they come alive through the irritation of their complementariness, by the mere fact that they are thrown together and must reckon with each other. Finally, they also in some sense absorb each other although their identities remain unchanged.

The situation in each *entremés* is the occasion for the fugal and dialectical encounters of such characters. They are supremely aware of being actors, of drawing on and out of one another the impulse of opposition, which stimulates the sense of their individuality. Like the various musical instruments in a jam session, they are alternately incited by one another to solo performances of unexpected virtuosity, and yet are constantly overtaken, merged, and absorbed by the racy dissonance of the whole ensemble playing together. One remembers the Soldier in *The Hawk-Eyed Sentinel,* more confident of his ability to ward off possible suitors than of the likelihood that he will win the scullery maid, whom he is compelled to resign at the end to the smug Sacristan. One thinks of the bickering councilmen, in *Choosing a Councilman in*

Daganzo, heatedly exchanging insults and pedantic quibbles, then giving the rustic candidates for office the occasion to demonstrate similar traits of their own. There is the dialectical interplay between each of the couples in *The Divorce-Court Judge*, mercilessly challenging each other's existence, but only, in effect, reinforcing it by their persistent assertiveness. The couples' incompatibility is amplified by the opportunity they are given to enumerate their grievances publicly in open court. But the fact that they agree to be judged helps to reinstate them in the community, against which individually they would seem to be rebelling. The status quo is thus maintained, and the principle of incompatibility is acknowledged only that it may be transcended by the social injunction. "That any truce, however short,/Beats the best divorce." A truce, not a settlement or resolution, is the note on which all the interludes end. Reality, which includes the incompatibility of individual wills, must be given its due, but the social injunction that checks it also dissolves for the moment all individual differences in the interludes.

The force of reality does not destroy the incompatibility principle, but absorbs it. Its dominance is upheld in the various interludes by an image of authority, which according to a law of comedy must intervene to redress absurdity and restore to the audience the commonsense view of society. And yet one observes several unexpected departures from this formula. In *The Divorce-Court Judge* and *Choosing a Councilman in Daganzo*, the formula is kept intact. In *Divorce* the Judge is the benign authority, and his rule triumphs at the end, as one would expect: even a shabby reconciliation is better than a divorce. In *Daganzo*, similarly, after a comic exposé of rustic follies, pretenses, and ignorance, the rule of the Council, sustained throughout by Cloven Hoof, the college graduate, is finally confirmed by the humanistic Peter Frog just after the intrusive Sacristan has been reproved for his impertinence.

In *Trampagos, the Pimp Who Lost His Moll,* the social norm is that of the underworld, closed in on itself, with its own code of conduct, which seems to ape the behavior of people in respectable society. The one intrusive note,

hardly louder than a whisper, occurs when a constable is
seen approaching. Then Trampagos is quick to allay the
gang's momentary consternation as the law passes by:
"The constable's a friend/ Of mine—no reason to be
scared of him./ . . .Suppose/ he'd stopped, he couldn't
nab us. I'm sure of that./ He'd never squawk, because
his palm's been greased." Subsequently, when Trampagos
takes the Preener as his new moll, the fortuitous appearance of the semilegendary master pimp Escarramán
puts the authoritative seal on the match, which closes the
play.

Another equivocal conclusion occurs in *The Basque Impostor* when the deluded whore Cristina is not only kept
from getting her due revenge on the pair who have
tricked her but is also forced to give them a good dinner
instead. Her vanity and cupidity are presumably more
culpable than the deceptiveness of the hoaxers.

In *The Wonder Show, The Cave of Salamanca,* and
The Jealous Old Husband, the image of authority is ac-
tually subverted. Chanfalla, the manager of the show,
closes the curtain on a pandemonium of deluded town
fathers fighting with an uninitiated quartermaster, and
Chanfalla's last speech suggests that the whole town is to
be hoodwinked in the same way on the following day. In
the *Cave* the equally guilty maid and her mistress—whose
assignations are interrupted, first by a poor student, then
by the returning husband—are gotten off the hook by the
vast credulity of the husband and his appetite for magical hocus-pocus. But the near-adulterers are not punished. In the *Husband* the compulsively watchful old
man is similarly betrayed and his wife left unpunished,
after her intimacies with the Gallant, because the husband's jealousy is apparently the greater folly. In each
instance the society restored at the end of the play looks
very much as it was at the start. The basic authority here
is not vested in a higher law, an abstract justice. It resides
in the particular character of individuals, who despite (or
because of) their crumbling follies, their designs on one
another, their conflicts and incompatibilities, not only
need but also choose to depend on one another.

If such characters are supremely aware of being actors, what keeps them from becoming merely histrionic,

flat, and unreal? The answer seems to be that they are
all caught up in the illusion that their world is real, that
they do not have to quarrel with it, and that they have
to demonstrate its actuality by being themselves, the individuals they were meant to be. Anything else—as, for
example, the assumption that they are grossly more or
less real than themselves—would be inadmissible on such
a stage. For to view them as simply inflated or deflated
types would give rise to a mistaken identification, the
sort of thing Cervantes had already ridiculed in the
Maese Pedro scene of *Don Quixote*. (There the fu-
rious Knight mounts the stage to destroy what he imagines are blasphemers of his ideal but who, when he cuts
them down, turn out to be sawdust and rag dolls.) The
lesson is that as soon as you interfere with the magical
distance safeguarding the illusion between audience and
actor, the indispensable illusion of reality turns to dust.
To discover how such a many-sided illusion comes about,
we must look at the sort of characters who are created to
embody it in the interludes.

III   To begin with, each character fills a social role
that is both typical and functional. In some instances
such roles are immediately discernible in the characters'
names. On the simplest level we have the identifying noun
—the Judge, the Old Man, the Porter, the Constable, and
so forth. On another level characters in their social
roles are mocked by some distinguishing attribute in their
names. A trio of whores are called Preener, Wagtail, and
Straybird. A quartet of councilmen are called Cloven
Hoof, Sneeze, Hardbread, and String Bean; the rustics,
who are candidates for office, are identified as Gassing,
Craggy, Hock, and Frog. Occasionally there is a folk-
loric figure, like Escarramán, the escaped prisoner,
after whom a popular dance is named—a character who
has only to put in an appearance and recite his history to
start the revel that concludes the interlude. Roque
Guinarde, a contemporary Robin Hood figure, does not
even appear, but is simply alluded to when a metaphor for

real benevolence is needed. Then there is the character with a ridiculous name (Trampagos, Chiquiznaque, Chanfalla, Aldonza de Minjaca), who actively takes on something of its absurdity in the part he plays. Servant girls, who are usually named Cristina, are typically lively, curious, young, and mischievous. Young wives with old or gullible husbands will have realistic names— Leonarda or Lorenza—and their husbands, ironically distorted common names, like Pancracio, which suggests something like "all-governing," or Cañizares, which by association with dried grass or reeds suggests "strawtubes."

As characters, the types they represent are centrally moved by the dialectics of the situation (the thematic matter) and by the need to act in opposition to other characters. So Cañizares, the deceived old husband, with perception whetted by jealousy, rises from dramatic typology to inveigh tellingly against his wife's confidante, Nettlesome, who stands for all neighbors. So, too, the Soldier overreaches his role as "the hawk-eyed sentinel" to show up the loutish Sacristan, who in fact defeats him. Where the folly hinges on flagrant superstition or ignorance, the main instigator (a stage manager or a neighbor) has only to appear and the gullible victims come swarming to him.

Through the interplay of characters in their thematic roles emerges the all-too-human situation in a typical action leading to dramatic revelation. In such an action the characters parody the roles of dupes and gulls, and because they are not seeking fulfillment or trying to achieve a serious purpose but are only pretending to do so, their words and behavior are not strictly ordained, as those of their counterparts in tragedy or romance would have to be. They can be more effectively themselves and freer—which is to say, individual and unique—because they are only going through the motions of being a type, a cog in a machine, a "somebody else." Something similar marks off Don Quixote and Sancho Panza. Each in his mock-serious quest (one to validate an anachronistic chivalric code, the other to leap an implacable class barrier and govern an island) becomes a dramatic character who bursts the typological mold in which he was cast, although in fact he has all along drawn his identity from it as a comic figure.

Nobody in the interludes is punished, nobody is rewarded, and everything turns out as it should be—that is, reconciled at the end, though only momentarily, to the way things are. Although the status quo prevails, something has been altered and revealed. How can this be, and how is it done? One might say that when the characters reveal themselves freely, they thereby reveal something intrinsic to drama: they reveal the fact that in the dramatic moment the artifice of reality does indeed become the desired reality; and so the illusion, with all its creaking machinery, momentarily displaces (i.e., becomes truer than) everyday reality.

The trick hinges on some threat to the established order, something mechanically initiated (the plot), and its consequence (the resolution) involves the restoration of the order. The trick, then, sets up a "well-ordered disorder" (*orden desordenada*), whose ready acceptability is a consequence of the audience's recognition that the art of illusion depends on nature itself being outdone.[1] Such maneuvering with illusion is borne out in the three interludes that would appeal most to a modern audience: *The Wonder Show, The Jealous Old Husband*, and *Trampagos, the Pimp Who Lost His Moll*. It is also basic in two others: *The Divorce-Court Judge* and *The Cave of*

---

[1] In *Don Quixote*, Part I, Chapter 50, the Knight is explaining the wondrous and irresistible fascinations to be found in books of chivalry: "Over there . . . an artfully wrought fountain of varicolored jasper and smoother marble; and there another of rustic design, with tiny clam shells and the twisted white and yellow houses of the snail arranged in a well-ordered disorder, mingled with bits of gleaming crystal and counterfeit emeralds, the whole forming a work in which art, imitating nature, would seem to have outdone the latter." The factitious and, in every sense of the word, fake paradise that Don Quixote so lovingly details may go a long way toward accounting for the wide appeal of his character—the disarming nature of Cervantes' central achievement in the novel—which, in turn, may fairly be described by the Knight's own words earlier in the chapter, where he alludes to books of chivalry in general: "books . . . which are read with general enjoyment and praised by the young and old alike, by rich and poor, the learned and the ignorant, the gentry and the plain people—in brief, by all sorts of persons of every condition and walk in life—do you mean to tell me that they are but lies?" (Excerpts translated by Samuel Putnam, *The Ingenious Gentleman, Don Quixote de la Mancha* (New York: The Viking Press, Inc., 1949), I, pp. 441–43.

Salamanca. In these plays some forbidden but cherished illusion intrudes to blur the circumstantial world of every-day life and momentarily raises it and the characters to a new—an exalted or special—view of themselves. This is traditionally the instigative element in farce, in which men's follies are played on in order to make them appear ridiculous. Yet in the Cervantes interludes the conventionally crude, dehumanizing attitude never creeps in. The kind of trick is sexual or magical or both, but in effect the dupes never really lose face; even their chastisement is minimal. As Cervantes puts it in *The Basque Impostor,* "A joke's not funny if it makes a person look contemptible." Contempt would degrade the character's humanity —an attitude Cervantes was temperamentally incapable of sustaining. Instead of roundly censuring or whipping his characters for their foibles, Cervantes involves them in the spell of an illusion that is larger than themselves. From this inescapable illusion they either emerge unchanged but better informed or, as in *The Wonder Show,* are swallowed at the end by the illusion.

In *The Wonder Show* the illusion is twofold and more intricate than it looks. For vanity's sake and to keep up appearances, the "better people" in town, the officials and their families, are constrained to accept the stage manager's conditions without question. To see the invisible tableau he has prepared, the audience must qualify by being legitimately born (not bastards) and pureblood Christians (not heretics). Anxious to prove themselves qualified, each tries to outdo the other by reacting to what he plainly does not see as though he were really experiencing it vividly with all his senses. The illusion here is that the better townspeople, who make up the inner audience, must pretend to see or imagine what is not there in order to be an audience at all. Outdoing the manager's initial deception, the last word in self-delusion comes when the Mayor has his compliant nephew mount the stage and dance with the invisible figure of Herodias—who made John the Baptist lose his head. The nephew, of course, simply gyrates alone, dancing with himself. The other side of the illusion is that when an intruder, the Quartermaster, enters, the audience refuses to return to the reality of their uninitiated lives but

incriminates the newcomer as a bastard and a heretic
for outrageously saying he cannot "see" the tableau. The
illusion has swallowed them and the curtain comes down
on the riotous dupes as the stage manager steps forth,
promising to take in the whole town in the same way at
the next performance. And yet it is not the illusion that
has triumphed so much as the folly of those who would
deliberately take it as reality in order to preserve the appearance of negative virtues—their not being bastards
and their not being heretics.

In *The Jealous Old Husband* there is another remark-
able illusion, although it is directed at only one character
while the others join together to sustain it, enact it, and
to some extent enjoy it. This occurs when the young Gallant is secretly hidden in the house of Lorenza, the love-
lorn wife, under the watchful eye of her old husband. A
neighbor lugs in a gigantic tapestry; in an appropriate
corner there is a full-sized representation of Rodamonte
the knight; the Gallant stands behind this and then slips
into Lorenza's room. Lorenza joins him there (though
presumably offstage) and realistically tells her husband
what is going on as she embraces the Gallant. The
trick is so bold and the husband so firmly convinced of
his own vigilant security that he is compelled to take the
reality as a delusion of his wife's, while on his side of
the door his young niece is frantically supporting the reality (till it becomes unclear whom she is abetting, the
husband or the wife) by urging her uncle to break down
the door. When he reluctantly threatens to do so, the
wife opens the door, hurls water in his face, and thereby
allows the Gallant to slip out unnoticed. Unlike the figure
of Herodias, the silent Gallant is visible to everyone except
the husband. Conveyed through an illusion (the tapestry), the punishing reality he represents does not
touch the husband. The husband is sunk in the illusion
that no male can get inside the house. In this he remains
deceived; he is simply made to apologize to Mistress
Nettlesome, his neighbor. But the audience, knowing
that she initiated the trick, can assume that the old
man's blind jealousy will be punished again and again.

Being what he is, he must continue to be duped by his own jealousy and deluded view of reality.[2]

In the *Trampagos* interlude the central illusion is that a company of pimps and whores share the sentimental virtues of respectable people, especially regarding the fidelity of husband and wife. And just when the point has been grandly secured, we witness a quick turn toward the more familiar underworld expediency of choosing a new moll for the widowed pimp.

In *The Divorce-Court Judge*—the shortest interlude and the only one that dispenses with a plot—the illusion overarching the complaints of the contentious couples is that the public airing of their grievances will bring about the desired divorce. But in actuality they thereby keep intact the legal machinery of the court, whose job is to remind them that all marriages are like pitched battles punctuated by brief truces.

In *The Cave of Salamanca* the husband's undisturbed gullibility fortifies the illusion when his idealized view of his wife's fidelity is shown to be the counterpart of his superstitious belief in magic.

What we get in these last brief products of Cervantes' genius is the extraordinary freedom of the characters to be themselves in a framework of considerable but not unlimited fluidity. There is nothing problematic in their makeup. In fact, because the problematic element is lacking, commentators who search for the means to aggrandize the author continually fill in the picture by suggesting biographical parallels to the plays and to the characters. It is as if the sense of felt life, the spectacle and play of vital existence insisting upon itself, were not enough, when it is, in fact, everything. In this regard, what Américo Castro, in discussing the basic theme of *Don Quixote*, calls "life as a process creative of itself" may also be applied to the eight interludes. For here too the value is existential, and the characters, "instead of

---

[2] An odd footnote to this particular form of high jinks is Cervantes' famous derogatory comment on translation in *Don Quixote* (Book II, Chapter 62). There he suggests how little he relishes such delusive operations when he says that reading a translation is "like looking at Flemish tapestries from the wrong side," where "though the figures are visible, they are full of threads that make them indistinct. . . ."

being logically arbitrary . . . become vitally valid, and we accept them not as farce or an amusement, but as one accepts all that appears authentic."

EDWIN HONIG
Brown University

Author's Prologue to the Reader*

I must beg your pardon, dearest reader, if in this Prologue you find me departing somewhat from my customary modesty. Several days ago I found myself among friends discussing the drama and related things, and these matters were treated with such subtlety and finesse that I thought the subject was brought to the point of utter perfection. There was also the question as to who was the first in Spain to take the drama out of its swaddling clothes and dress it up under a canopy in gala costume. I, as the oldest man present, said I remembered the performances by the great Lope de Rueda, a man as distinguished for his acting as for his good sense. Born in Seville, he was a gold beater by trade—that is, one of those employed in making gold leaf. His pastoral poetry was admirable, and no one then or since has equaled him in this vein. Although I was only a boy then and could not properly judge the excellence of his verse, I find, on the basis of some lines of his that have stayed with me, that now as a mature person I was right in holding that opinion. And if it were not beyond the purpose of this Prologue, I would quote some verses here to illustrate the truth of what I say.

In the days of that famous Spaniard, an actor-manager's whole stock was put into one sack, made up of four white sheepskins adorned with gilt leather, four beards and wigs, and four shepherd's crooks more or less. The plays were colloquies in the form of eclogues spoken by two or three shepherds and a shepherdess. These were

* From *Ocho Comedias y Ocho Entremeses Nuevos. Nunca representados* (1615), Miguel de Cervantes Saavedra.

then embellished and expanded with two or three interludes—now about a Negress or a Ruffian, now about a
Clown or a Basque, and all four parts, not to mention
many others, were played by this same man Lope with
the greatest imaginable skill and sense of decorum.
There were no stage effects in those days, no set-tos between Moors and Christians, either on foot or on horseback. Nor did any sort of character emerge or seem to
emerge from the bowels of the earth under the stage.
The stage itself consisted of four benches in a square
with four to six planks placed upon them, four spans
high off the ground. Nor were there any clouds with
angels or spirits descending from heaven. The only stage
device was an old blanket drawn both ways by cords,
allowing for what is now called the dressing room. Behind this were the musicians, singing some old ballad
without guitar accompaniment. Lope de Rueda died, and,
as he was such a famous and excellent person, was buried
in the Cathedral at Córdoba (the city where he died)
between the two choirs. Luis López, the well-known
madman, is also buried there.

Following Lope de Rueda came Navarro, a native of
Toledo. He was famous in the role of the cowardly ruffian.
He developed the dramatic stage a bit more and used
boxes and trunks for his wardrobe instead of the old
sack of clothes. He took the singers out and put them in
front of the blanket in the public theater; he had the
players take off their beards (who until then never
played a role without a false beard) and made them all
act barefaced, except for those who took the parts of old
men and others who required such facial disguise. He
invented the physical effects of clouds, thunder and
lightning, and duels and battles, though he did not bring
these things to the sublime heights we know today.

And now there is one fact that nobody can gainsay—
and here I must seem to exceed the bounds of modesty
—namely, that in my own plays, *The Commerce of Al-
giers, The Siege of Numantia,* and *The Naval Battle,* then
produced in the Madrid theaters, it was seen that I had
boldly reduced the conventional five-act play to three
acts. I showed or, as it would be better to say, I was
the first to dramatize the secret thoughts and yearnings

of the heart by bringing moral personifications on the stage, to the general and welcome applause of an audience. In those days I wrote twenty to thirty plays, and all of them were put on the boards without provoking the offerings of such votive gifts as cucumbers or other missiles of the sort. The plays ran their course without inciting hisses, catcalls, or riots. But having other things to do that occupied me then, I abandoned my pen and the writing of plays, and thereupon appeared the monster of nature, the great Lope de Vega, who ran off with the crown of drama. He made vassals of all the players, putting everyone under his dominion. He filled the world with his own happy, well-wrought plays. And, however many he wrote (now exceeding ten thousand pages in length, which is one of the great things that may be said about them), all have been seen on the stage or at least all have been produced, according to what one hears said of them. And of those other dramatists, of whom there are many, who wished to compete with him and receive their share of glory, all of these put together have not written half of what he has written alone.

But, although God does not endow everyone with everything, one should not for this reason overlook the worthiness of those works by Doctor Ramón, which were the most numerous after those of the great Lope, nor underestimate those most highly skillful contrivances of Miguel Sánchez, nor the gravity of Doctor Mira de Mescua, who brings singular honor to our nation, nor the discreet and prodigal speculativeness of Canon Tárraga, nor the sweetness and gentility of Don Guillén de Castro, the wit of Aguilar, the lustrous and tumultuous grandeur and resonance in the plays of Luis Vélez de Guevara, nor those that are now in the making by the sharply ingenious Don Antonio de Galarza, nor the promising future shown in *The Shady Games of Love* by Gaspar de Ávila. For together with the great Lope, all these men and several others have helped to establish a gigantic body of dramatic work.

Some years ago I returned to my old pastime, and thinking the times were still the same as when they sang my praises, I again began to write a few plays. But I found no birds in last year's nests—I mean, I found no managers who wanted them, although they knew I had them. And so, I put them away in a trunk, consecrating and condemning them to eternal silence. In good time a bookseller told me he might buy them from me, although a royally licensed stage manager had told him that a good deal could be expected from my prose, but from my poetry, nothing at all. To tell the truth, I was certainly pained to hear this, and I said to myself, "Either I have changed and become another person or the times have improved immensely—which is generally the other way around, since people always praise the days gone by." I went back to glance through my plays and some of the interludes with which they had been put away, and I judged neither kind to be so bad as not to deserve being brought out of the obscurity in which that clever manager had cast them and into the purview of other less finicky and more understanding managers. I grew tired of it all and sold them to the same bookseller who has published them in the imprint now offered you here. He paid me a modest sum; I took the money agreeably, without having to haggle with actors and managers. I wish the plays were the best in the world, or at least reasonably good. You will be the judge of that, dear reader. And if you find anything good in them, contrary to what that stage-manager critic of mine says, tell him to amend his criticism, since I offend nobody; and tell him to note that they do not contain any patent or covert sort of stupidity. The verse is just what is called for in these plays and is of necessity written in the low style, the only one of the three styles that is possible. The language of the interludes is appropriate to the characters presented in them. And if he amends his views in regard to all this, I will offer him a play I am now writing, called *The Deception in Plain View,* which, if I do not deceive myself, should make him happy. And so with that, God give you health and me patience.

THE
DIVORCE-COURT
JUDGE

(El Juez de los Divorcios)

CAST

Judge
Clerk
Prosecutor
Old Man
Mariana, his wife
Soldier

Doña Guiomar, his wife
Doctor
Aldonza de Minjaca, his
    wife
Porter
Two Musicians

The Divorce-Court Judge

*Enter the Judge, with two others: the Clerk and
the Prosecutor. He takes his place on a bench.
Enter the little Old Man and Mariana, his wife.*

Mariana. Good, there's the Divorce-Court Judge on his
bench. So now I must have it settled, one way or the
other. From now on, I must have my freedom, like a hawk
that's free of duties and taxes.

Old Man. For the love of God, Mariana, don't set up
such a howl about your private affairs. Please lower your
voice, for God's sake. Look how you've roused all the
neighbors with your outbursts! Now that you're in court,
you can at least tell it to the Judge without shouting.

Judge. My good people, what quarrel brings you here?

Mariana. Your Honor: a divorce, I want a divorce! I'll
say it again and again and again! I want a divorce, a divorce, a divorce!

Judge. But, madam, from whom and for what reason?

Mariana. From whom? From this old dotard.

Judge. Why?

Mariana. Because I can't stand his pestering, and always
having to take care of his endless ailments. Because my
parents didn't raise me to be a hospital attendant or a
sick nurse. It was a good fat dowry I brought to this
bag of bones who's been eating my life away. When I
fell into his clutches, my face was smooth and bright
as a mirror, and now it's as rough a blanket. Your
Honor, dear Judge, divorce me, unless you want me to

29

hang myself. Look, look at the wrinkles on this face—
and all because of the tears I shed every day since I
married this mummy.

Judge. Don't weep, madam. Lower your voice and dry
your tears. I'll see you get justice here.

Mariana. Your Honor, let me weep. It's my only comfort. In sensible kingdoms and commonwealths, they'd
set a time limit on marriage. Every three years they'd
dissolve or renew it, like a lease, instead of letting it last
a lifetime to the endless sorrow of both parties.

Judge. If such an arrangement could or should be made
practical, especially if money would do the trick, it would
have been done long ago. But, madam, let me know more
precisely why you want a divorce.

Mariana. Age—his cold December against my warm
and early May; my sleep broken at midnight when I
have to heat towels and make poultices for his kidneys;
my having to wrap him up in one truss after another, instead of trussing him to a stake, which is what he deserves; all that to-do at night about putting those syrups
and sedatives near him so he doesn't choke on his own
spittle; and then my having to stand that rotten smell
that comes out of his mouth and stinks for miles
around.

Clerk. Some sort of rotting molar, no doubt.

Old Man. Impossible! There's not one molar or any
damned tooth at all left in my mouth!

Prosecutor. And yet there's a law, as I understand it,
that says that bad breath constitutes sufficient grounds
for divorce between a husband and a wife, and vice
versa.

Old Man. The fact is, gentlemen, the bad breath she
imputes to me derives not from rotten molars (and mine
are long since gone), nor even less from my stomach
(which is perfectly sound), but from the evil in her own
heart. Gentlemen, you don't know this woman. If you
knew her, you'd reel back in horror and have to cross
yourselves in self-defense. For twenty-two martyred

years now I've lived with her, and never once have I complained of her insults, her outbursts, and her fits. And now it's going on two years that she's been pushing and dragging me to my grave so that I'm half deaf with her yelling and driven out of my mind with her abuse. If she nurses me, as she says, she does it spitefully. A nurse's touch should be soft and gentle. To sum it up, gentlemen, I'm the one dying on her account and she's the one flourishing on mine—because that woman controls everything I own, lock, stock and barrel.

Mariana. Everything you own? What do you really own that does not come out of the profits you made on my dowry? Besides, half the estate since we got married belongs to me, whether you like it or not. And if I dropped dead this minute, you wouldn't get a red cent of it—that's just how much I care for you.

Judge. Tell me this, sir: when you were committed to matrimonial relations with your wife, were you vigorous —in good spirits and good health?

Old Man. As I've said, it's been twenty-two years since I was committed to her, like a galley slave sentenced to row under the cruelest slave driver, though when I married her I was in my prime and could always match her, bid for bid.

Mariana. Every cock crows on his own dung pile.

Judge. Silence, silence! Hold your tongue, woman, and go on home. I find no reason to divorce you. Take the chaff with the wheat. You can't make a husband stop time in its flight or keep it from rushing by and sweeping his youth away. Discount present disabilities and think of the good times he gave you when he could. And now, not another word out of you.

Old Man. If possible, I'd consider it a great favor if your Honor would relieve my misery and lead me out of this bondage. Otherwise, if you leave me as I now am, at the breaking point, you are turning me over to an executioner who's about to hang me. If you won't divorce us, let's compromise: shut her up in a convent and me in a monastery; we'll divide our estate and then spend what's left of our lives in peace serving God.

Mariana. Over my dead body! Coop me up in a convent? You think I'm some shy young thing who likes screens, bars, grilled windows, and watchmen? Shut yourself up because *you* can stand it—you who have no eyes to see, no ears to hear, no feet to walk on, and no fingers to feel anything with. As for me, I'm still healthy, with all my senses keen and alert. I want to enjoy them openly, not hide them in the dark or bury them like an ace in a hole.

Clerk. There's a wild woman for you!

Prosecutor. And the husband so sensible—but worn out.

Judge. Well, I can't grant this divorce, *quia nullam invenio causam*—since I find no grounds for it.

> *Enter a Soldier in parade dress, with his wife,*
> *Doña Guiomar.*

Guiomar. Thank God for granting my wish and bringing me before your Honor. I beg you, with all my heart and soul, to divorce me from this one.

Judge. What do you mean, *this one?* Doesn't he have a name? You might at least say *from this man.*

Guiomar. If he were a man, I wouldn't be trying to divorce him.

Judge. Well, then, what is he?

Guiomar. A block of wood.

Soldier (*aside*). By God, I must really be made of wood to take this silently. But maybe if I don't defend myself or answer the woman, the Judge will be inclined to condemn me; and so, while he thinks he's punishing me he'll really be freeing me, miraculously, like a slave out of the Turkish dungeons.

Prosecutor. Control yourself, woman. Tell your story without insulting your husband so that the Judge of the Divorce Court, now sitting before you, can weigh the merits of your case without prejudice.

Guiomar. Then you don't want me to call this dummy a block of wood when there's no more life to him than there is in a log?

Mariana. She and I really have the same grievance.

Guiomar. I tell you, sir, I married this man, since your Honor insists I call him one, though this is not the man I married.

Judge. How's that? I don't understand.

Guiomar. I mean that I thought I'd married a man who was burning and churning, but in a few days I discovered I'd married a block, as I just said. Because he doesn't know his right hand from his left, and he has no way of earning a few cents to support the house and family. He fritters the mornings away at Mass and hanging around the Guadalajara gate gossiping, picking up the latest news, telling and listening to lies. Afternoons, and mornings too, sometimes, he goes off to the gambling dens and joins the riffraff and hangers-on, who, I'm told, are the kind of people the gamblers detest like the plague. At two o'clock he comes home to eat without having got a single miserable tip because it's now out of fashion for the winners to give any. Then he breezes out again, comes back at midnight, eats if he finds anything to eat, and if not, crosses himself, yawns, and goes to bed. Then all night long he's never still a minute—twisting and squirming. I ask him what's wrong. He tells me he's composing a sonnet in his head for a friend who's asked him to write one. So he puts on airs of being a poet, as if that were some sort of job in itself, outside of all worldly necessities.

Soldier. In everything she's told you, my wife, Doña Guiomar, has not strayed a jot from the strait and narrow course of truth. And if I were less justified in what I do than she in what she says, I'd long since have sucked up to the right people here and there, got hold of a traveling-magistrate's staff, and made my way, like all those sharp little hustlers and bustlers: staff in hand, astride an ornery, stunted, hired old mule, though without a mule boy at my side, since such mules are rented only because they're worn out and perfectly useless.

There I'd go, with those little saddlebags strapped behind, one containing a collar and shirt, the other some cheese, some bread, and a skin of wine, and the only change of clothes I'd make for the journey would be to put on a pair of leggings and one spur. And with my assignment and an itch on my chest, I'd go clomping over the Toledo Bridge, grumbling to my sluggish mule, and after a few days send home a slab of bacon and a few yards of unbleached linen—in short, the cheapest sort of stuff made in the district of my assignment—and on that I'd support my family, as only the worst sinner can. But since I have no trade or profession, and since gentlemen won't take me on because I'm married, I don't know what to do with myself. As for the country squires, they're so poor it's impossible to deal with them. And so, because I have no choice, and as my wife wishes it, I must beg your Honor to separate and divorce us.

Guiomar. And there's more to it than that, your Honor. Seeing that my husband is such an empty-handed good-for-nothing, I've tried my hardest to help him but cannot do it, for after all, I am an honest woman and I won't do anything that smacks of indecency.

Soldier. That's just why this woman deserves to be cherished, except that behind her lily-white honor is the ugliest disposition on earth. She's madly jealous, given to sudden outbursts and fits of idle pretensions, and because I'm so poor, she treats me like mud under her feet. But worst of all, your Honor, is that simply because she's faithful to me she takes it for granted I'll put up with every rude and nasty word she utters.

Guiomar. And why not? Why shouldn't you treat me decently and respectfully when I'm so virtuous?

Soldier. Listen, Guiomar. Here, before these gentlemen, I'd like to ask you this: why do you burden me with your virtue when it's your simple duty to be virtuous anyway? You owe it to your good parents, to your Christian upbringing, and to your own conscience. It's strange that women want their husbands to respect them for being virtuous and faithful, as if their whole perfection were simply a matter of their being so. Meanwhile they disregard the chinks in their armor where a thousand finer virtues leak out. What do I care about your high-falutin decency when you don't insist on it in your maid and when you're always shuffling around scowling, grouchy, jealous, suspicious, wasteful, moody, lazy, quarrelsome, grumbling, plus all the other petty vices— enough to eat the heart out of two hundred husbands? And yet in spite of all this, your Honor, I'd never say my wife is guilty of any personal defect, and I confess I'm a block of wood, lazy, incompetent, good-for-nothing. And so, on the grounds of common sense, if no other, your Honor must separate us. To put it quite plainly, I have no defense against what my wife has said. I consider the case closed and am happy to stand condemned.

Guiomar. What possible defense *could* you have against my charges? You bring nothing home to feed me or my servant. And how many servants do I have? Just one, and she so skinny that what she eats would starve a grasshopper.

Clerk. That's enough. Make way for the other petitioners.

> *Enter a man dressed as a Doctor—who is really a bonesetter—and Aldonza de Minjaca, his wife.*

Doctor. I have four good and sufficient reasons why your Honor should divorce me from my wife here, Doña Aldonza de Minjaca.

Judge. Your mind's all made up, is it? State your four reasons.

Doctor. First, because I can't stand the sight of her any more than I could a devil out of hell. Second, because she herself knows why. Third, for a reason I'd blush to tell. Fourth, because the devil himself will fly off with my soul when I die if I have to spend the rest of my life with her.

Prosecutor. He's made his case superabundantly clear!

Minjaca. Your Honor, please listen to me and consider this: if my husband has four grounds for divorce, I have four hundred. First, because every time I look at him I tell myself, "That's the Old Harry himself." Second, be-

cause I was deceived when I married him: he said he was
a real doctor but he turned out to be a quack, a bone-
setter who fixes splints and treats slight ailments, and
not a regular doctor at all. Third, because he's jealous of
the very sunlight that touches me. Fourth, because I can't
bear the sight of him and want to be a million miles
away. . . .

Clerk.   How in the world can anyone fix these clocks
when their wheels run every which way?

Minjaca.   In the fifth place——

Judge.   Here, here, madam. If you think you can stand
there and give me all your four hundred reasons, you've
got another guess coming. I'm in no mood to hear you
out, and there's no time for it here. Your case will be
taken under advisement, so good-bye. We've other business to attend to.

Doctor.   What further evidence do you need than that
I don't want to die with her and she doesn't want to live
with me?

Judge.   If those were sufficient grounds for divorce, un-
told millions would now be shrugging off the yoke of
matrimony.

> *Enter a Porter, wearing a four-cornered pointed
> hood, varicolored, attached to his cape.*

Porter.   Your Honor, I'm just a porter, I don't deny it
—but I'm a pureblood Christian (not one of your con-
verts) and an honest, respectable man, you can be sure
of that. If I didn't sometimes take a drop of wine too
much, or it takes me (which is truer), I'd be head man
in our brotherhood of charcoal carriers by now. But aside
from that (though there's lots more to say on that score),
I want the good Judge to know that once, while I was
polluted sick, I promised to marry a fallen woman. When
I was sober again, I kept my promise, married the woman, and saved her from a life of sin. I bought her a stall
in the market, and now she's got so stuck up and nasty
that there's nobody who comes to her stall she doesn't
quarrel with, either about short-weighting them or about
somebody touching the fruit. And like as not, she picks

up a weight and chucks it at their heads or wherever she happens to hit. And she tears into their family, four generations back, and is never for a moment at peace with her neighbors, near and far, and I've got to keep my sword sliding in and out like a trombone all day long, just to defend her, and we never earn enough to pay the fines for selling underweight or the damages for assault and battery. If possible, I'd like your Honor to separate us or, at least, to slow her down so she'll be a bit more easy and gentle. And if you do that, I promise your Honor to carry gratis, on this back of mine, all the coal you buy this summer—and I have a pretty good reputation among the hired porters.

Doctor.   I know the good man's wife. She's just as mean as my Aldonza; I can't think of anything worse.

Judge.   Look here, my good people. Though some of you have given a few good reasons that may warrant a divorce, you'll have to put them down in writing and have them attested to by witnesses. Then I'll take all your cases under advisement. . . . But what's this? Music and guitars in my courtroom? That's quite a novelty!

Enter two Musicians.

Musician.   Your Honor, we have been sent by that quarrelsome couple you subdued, pacified, and reconciled the other day. They're now celebrating their reunion with a feast at home, and they've sent us to beg you to honor them with your presence.

Judge.   That I shall do with all my heart, and wish to heaven all of you here would follow their example.

Prosecutor.   If they did, we lawyers and clerks would starve to death. No, no! Let everyone sue for divorce. Because in the end, I say in the end, most of them end up by staying married while we reap the benefits of their quarrels and follies.

Musician.   Well, let's begin our revels right here and now.

The Musicians sing:

Tell decent couples who perforce

Become the quarreling sort
That any truce, however short,
Beats the best divorce.

Unless the couple's really drowned
In blind stupidity,
They know a spat on St. John's Day
Brings peace the year around.

Then loving-kindness, in due course,
Awakes, and they are taught
That any truce, however short,
Beats the best divorce.

However wild their jealous eyes,
However dark their fears,
There glows through lovely women's tears
A kind of paradise.

And Cupid thinks so too, the boss
Of love of every sort:
That any truce, however short,
Beats the best divorce.

TRAMPAGOS, THE PIMP WHO LOST HIS MOLL

(El Rufián Viudo, Llamado Trampagos)

CAST

Trampagos, pimp

Vademecum, his servant

Chiquiznaque, pimp

Johnny Brights (Juan Claros), pimp

The Preener (La Repulida), whore

The Wagtail (La Pizpita), whore

The Straybird (La Mostrenca), whore

Escarramán, escaped prisoner

Person, a man

Two Barber-Musicians

Trampagos, the Pimp Who Lost His Moll

*Enter Trampagos in a mourning cloak, and with him
Vademecum, his servant, with two foils.*

Trampagos. Vademecum!

Vademecum.   Sir?

Trampagos.   You have the foils?

Vademecum. Right here.

Trampagos.   Good, hand them over—now then, move.
Bring out the chair that's got a back to it.
Also, bring all the other seats out here.

Vademecum. What seats? Do we, by any chance, have
one?

Trampagos. Well, bring the mortar box and fencing
shield,
You lout, and that bench we use to prop the mattress.

Vademecum. The thing is damaged; one of the legs is
missing.

Trampagos. You call that damaged?

Vademecum.   I wouldn't overlook it.

                                Exit Vademecum.

Trampagos. Ah, Pericona, Pericona! Mine
And everybody else's Pericona!
Your time ran out at last. I'm left behind,
You're gone—the worst of it is, I don't know where.

Ah, well, considering the way you lived,
The pious thing would be to hope you dwell
Among—but I don't have the strength of mind
To say where you should dwell in the next world.
Now that you're gone, my life will be a sort
Of living death. Oh, why was I not standing
At your bedside when you breathed your last?
I might have caught your spirit as it fled
And given it a home in my warm stomach! . . .
O wretched human destiny, no one
Can ever trust you! "I, who yesterday
Was Pericona, am cold earth today,"
Just as that celebrated poet said.

> *Enter Chiquiznaque, pimp.*

Chiquiznaque.   Trampagos boy, what's this, have you become
Your own worst enemy? The shining star
Of our whole gang takes the veil and shrouds
Himself inside a mourning coat! Trampagos
Boy, it's time you quit the groaning and
The sighing. Take all your flowing tears and turn
Them into alms for prayers and Masses for
Great Pericona's soul—God keep her now.
That'll do more good than tears and sniffles.

Trampagos.   Chiquiznaque, now you're gabbling like
A theologian. Come on, and while I'm patching
Up my life again let's you and me
Try gabbling something new with these.

Chiquiznaque.   Now's not
The time for thrusts, Trampagos. Gusts and floods
Of rich condolences will soon pour in—
Why bother with these sword tricks?

> *Enter Vademecum with the chair, very old
> and broken down.*

Vademecum.   Ah, yes. Just keep my master off his thrusts
And stances, and I swear he'd just as soon
Be dead.

Trampagos.   Now go get the mortar and the bench.
And, Vademecum, don't forget the shield.

Vademecum.   Why not the rest—the spit, the plates, the
    frypan?

Exit again.

Trampagos.   Later we'll talk about this fencing trick
    Of mine—it's new, I tell you, there's nothing like it.
    But for the moment, my darling angel's death
    Has queered me, tied my hands, and numbed my brain.

Chiquiznaque.   How old was she, poor woman?

Trampagos.   Among her friends
    And neighbors, she passed for thirty-two.

Chiquiznaque.
                                            Still in
    Her prime!

Trampagos.   But she was fifty-six, to tell
    The truth. Still, I must give her credit: she knew
    Just how to hide her age. She was a wizard
    At touching up white hair. And the knack she had
    For turning silver ringlets golden! The sixth
    Day of next month makes fifteen years she was
    My mainstay and support, and not once in all
    That time got me in a brawl or even
    Brought me close to getting flogged. So if
    My count is right, it's been fifteen Lenten
    Seasons since the day the poor thing first
    Became my precious everloving moll.
    Since all those Lents fell on her head, she must
    Have had her ear bent by the droning out
    Of thirty sermons, if not more, and still
    She had the guts, for my sake, to resist
    Them all. She stood there like a rock against
    The crashing waves and sea. How many times
    The poor thing underwent that crazy siege
    Of yelling pleas and prayers, and then, soaked through
    And through with sweat she'd come to me and say,
    "Trampagos, dear, if only Heaven would
    Deduct some of my sins because of all
    I have to suffer for you, oh my sweet!"

Chiquiznaque.   What courage, what stupendous con-
    stancy!

She'll surely be rewarded for it!

Trampagos.   I wouldn't
Doubt it. Listening to that pious stuff
And never squeezing out a single tear.
You'd think she had a soul of wood or flint.

Chiquiznaque.   A dame like that deserves to have her name
In marble, the way the Greeks and Romans did it.
What killed her?

Trampagos.   Killed her? Nothing much. Bad liver,
The doctors said, and then a fit of gas.
They said that if she'd only drunk water
Of tamarisk for seventy years, she would
Have stayed alive.

Chiquiznaque.   She didn't take it?

Trampagos.   No,
She died instead.

Chiquiznaque.   She was a fool. Just think,
If she had drunk it steadily, she could
Have lived till Judgment Day. But they were wrong,
Not giving her the sweat cure.

Trampagos.   No, they did—
Eleven times.

Vademecum returns with the aforementioned seats.

Chiquiznaque.   And did that help her?

Trampagos.   Almost
Every time. She was like a green
Tomato afterward, tough as some
Old pear or wild crab-apple tree.

Chiquiznaque.   I hear
She had a lot of running sores over
Her arms and legs.

Trampagos.   The poor girl's body gushed
Like fountains in the royal park. And yet,
The so-called earth, which feeds on her today,
Consumes in her the whitest, fairest flesh

It ever has devoured. Embracing her—
If you discount her breath, which started in
To stink two years ago—embracing her
Was just like taking in your arms a pot of
Sweet basil or carnations.

Chiquiznaque.   Caries or cankers
Probably attacked her pearly mouth—
I mean her teeth and molars.

Trampagos.   She woke one day
And found them gone.

Vademecum.   And that's a fact—also
The reason was she went to bed without them.
Once I counted five that were her own,
And twelve she hid inside her maw were false.

Trampagos.   Liar! Who asked you for your opinion?

Vademecum.   It's just the honest truth.

Trampagos.   Chiquiznaque,
I've got it—that feint we used to practice, it's just
Come back to me. Pick up a foil and take
The first position.

Vademecum.   Hold it there, don't make
Another move: the gang is flocking to
The lure. Now here's the Preener and the Wagtail,
And Straybird and that bruiser, Johnny Brights.

Trampagos.   They're more than welcome here—come in,
come in.

*Enter The Preener, The Wagtail, The Straybird, and the
pimp Johnny Brights.*

Johnny.   Greetings to you and thanks, Trampagos boy.

Preener.   God lift your gloom and flood your heart with
light!

Wagtail.   And strip you of that awful mourning coat!

Straybird.   God, what a spook! Take him away!

Vademecum.   What manners!

Trampagos.   I'd have to be a Polyphemus-cave-man-

Anthropophagus-and-heartless-ape-
Wild-Indian-man-eating-alligator
To let myself wear anything but black
On such a sad occasion.

Johnny.   True enough!

Trampagos.   To me she was the richest silver mine
In Potosí, the rampart that the ivy
Of my every weakness clung to, the tree
Whose shade cooled all of my anxieties.

Johnny.   That Pericona was a mine of gold.

Trampagos.   Just sitting there from nightfall till the time
They shut the house doors, then finding I was richer
By sixty copper pieces—that was nothing
To spit at, you agree? Well, it's all gone,
Gone down the hole she rots in now.

Preener.   I must
Admit I'm sinful guilty: I always used
To envy her wonderful efficiency.
I can't beat her at that—I do the best
I can, but it's not all I'd like to do.

Wagtail.   Don't let that trouble you. It's better having
God on your side than rising early in
The morning. You get my point, I'm sure.

Vademecum.   You spit
Those proverbs out like cherry stones. I hope
God sees to it they comfort you in bed,
You sluts!

Straybird.   We are what we are, and God
Helps those who help themselves. I can't complain.
I eat my three square meals a day and see
My fancy man is dressed to kill. As long
As she's got spunk, no woman need be ugly.
The devil's ugly.

Vademecum.   That's it, Straybird, stand up
For your rights; you do it well. You'd do
It better if you also said you're just
A sweet young thing, because you are, and then some.

Chiquiznaque.   Look at Trampagos. He's a sorry sight
  Indeed.

Trampagos.   These lamps of mine, after I donned
  This cloak, became two weeping stills.

Vademecum.   Of liquor?

Trampagos.   Oh, do I drip so much—son of a witch?

Vademecum.   Why, you can drip enough to satisfy
  Four washerwomen under the city bridge
  And nearly fill their colanders besides.
  But what else would you drip if not hot liquor?

Johnny.   As I see it, the great Trampagos ought
  To stop this endless weepiness and go
  Back to the *sicut erat in principio,*
  I mean his old-time happy self, throw off
  This dismal mourning rag, and find himself
  A brand-new piece. A living man needs bread,
  I say, so let the dead bury the dead.

Preener.   This Johnny Brights jaws like a Latinist.

Wagtail.   I may be small, Trampagos, but my will
  To please you is tremendous. I don't have
  A man, but I've got eighty silver coins.

Preener.   I'm ready with a hundred—and I'm *fast.*

Straybird.   I'm twenty-two or so—and no one's fool!

Preener.   Jesus, what's this? Are you ganging up
  Against me, Wagtail, Straybird? You think you'll beat
  Me in an open field, do you? You
  Snake-in-the-box, and you, you little runt!

Wagtail.   Well, by my granny Mary Booby's bones,
  Just listen to that dried-up apple! Know what
  I think of you, you worthless piece of foreign
  Money? Just look at her, the lousy primped-up
  Nobody, trying to lord it over us!

Straybird.   Not over me, I'll have you know. No one
  Lords me until he fits and suits me right!

Johnny.   On guard. I am the Wagtail's champion!

Chiquiznaque.   I'm for you. Preener's under my wing
  now.

Vademecum. So now they'll slice each other up like
    Trojans!
  They're pulling out their yellow butcher knives.
  I say—just like that Trojan War again!

Preener. No one need defend me, Chiquiznaque.
  With these two sinful hands of mine, I'll take
  My own revenge and tear this twisted little
  Yellow-bellied quince face into shreds!

Johnny. Now, Preener, leave this to great Johnny
    Brights.

Wagtail. Just let her try it once. Just let me at
  That piece of lumpy dough she calls her face.

Enter a very excited Person.

Person. Police, police, John Brights! The constable
  Is turning up this street.

                        Exit immediately.

Johnny.   Son of a gun!
  I'm taking off!

Trampagos.   Now hold on, everyone,
  And just keep cool. The constable's a friend
  Of mine—no reason to be scared of him.

Enter the Person Again.

Person. He won't stop here; he's only passing by.

                                  Exit.

Chiquiznaque. He had me shivering in my boots that
    time.
  I'm supposed to be in exile.

Trampagos.   Suppose
  He'd stopped, he couldn't nab us. I'm sure of that.
  He'd never squawk, because his palm's been greased.

Vademecum. Stop brawling, then, and let my master
    choose
  The piece that squares or dovetails with him best.

Preener. I'm satisfied.

Wagtail.   And so am I.

Straybird.   Me too.

Vademecum.   That's strategy—thank God I got them
   Settled down.

Trampagos.   My heart's not in it but I'll choose.

Straybird.   God help you.

Preener.   Trampagos, if you're slack, you're sure
   To choose a slacker.

Trampagos.   That was a slip. I won't
   Be slack. Here goes.

Straybird.   God help you.

Trampagos.   Then, I say—
   I hereby choose the Preener!

Johnny.   He's made his bed,
   Chiquiznaque—let him lie in it.

Chiquiznaque.   Bed or no bed, he sure picked something
   luscious.

Preener.   I'm yours. Come brand me as your slave on
   Both these cheeks.

Wagtail.   The witch!

Straybird.   Sheer luck. Don't envy her.
   Trampagos has no morals. One day he buries
   Pericona, the next day he forgets her.

Preener.   That's very true.

Trampagos.   Vademecum, wrap up
   This cloak and get the cathouse cop to cough up
   Twelve *reales* for it.

Vademecum.   I'll get fourteen.

Trampagos.   Go on, now—move. And bring three gallons
   Back of that expensive stuff. Now flap your feet
   Like wings.

Vademecum.   My shoulders too.

      Exit Vademecum with the cloak, leaving Trampagos in
                             his doublet.

Trampagos.   I swear that if
   I had to wear that cloak another moment,
   I'd be dead and buried in the morning.

Preener.   My, this is daylight to my eyes (which now
   are yours). And how much nicer now you look
   Without that heavy, sickly mourning cloak!

           Enter two Musicians without guitars.

First Musician.   My chum and I smelled wine, so in we
   came.

Trampagos.   You're welcome. And your guitars?

First Musician.   They're in the shop.
   Let Vademecum get them.

Second Musician.   Yes, let him . . .
   No, better—I'll get them myself.

                                        Leaving.

First Musician.   And while
   You're on your way go tell my better half
   If someone wants his hair snipped, have him wait
   A little. I'll only take a drop or two,
   Whip through some choruses, and then come back.
   It looks as if Trampagos were himself
   Again, and spoiling for a bit of fun.

               Enter Vademecum.

Vademecum.   I left the jug out there in the entry.

Trampagos.   Well, bring it in.

Vademecum.   There are no cups.

Trampagos.   What's wrong
   With you? The chamber pot's hardly been used
   Yet. Go fetch it. Well, get the devil out
   Of here. You'd disgrace a duke, the way
   You carry on.

Vademecum.   Don't upset yourself.
   I'll find some containers—even if
   They're only hats.

                    (*Aside.*) This chap's a hypocrite!
Enter a man dressed as a prisoner, with a chain over

his shoulder; he begins to stare fixedly at everyone,
and they return the stare.

Preener.   Good Lord, is this a ghost? Or what is it?
Don't tell me it's Escarramán? Of course
It is. Escarramán, my love, come hold
Me in your arms, my sweet, and mastermind
Of all the underworld!

Trampagos.   Escarramán,
Old boy, what's this? You stand there like a statue.
Open up and speak. We're all friends here.

Wagtail.   What sort of get-up are you in, and why
The chain? Now, really, you're no ghost. When I
Touch you, it's flesh and blood I feel.

Straybird.   My dear,
That's him, all right—he can't deny it, mum
Though he may be.

Escarramán.   My name's Escarramán.
Now listen to my story, I'll make it brief.

The Barber-Musician returns with two guitars and gives
one to his companion.

An angry judge condemned me to a galley,
Where I was outside lead man of the gang
When we shipwrecked off Barbary. There
I had a change of luck and captors. The Turks
Kept me a slave two months, and then, thank God,
I found a small boat to escape in. So
I got my liberty; now I'm a man
Again. I made a vow and swore never
To take these clothes or burden off until
I'd hung them on the sacred walls of San
Millán, the holy hermitage in my
Hometown. Now that's the gist of all that's worth
Remembering about my life abroad.
What is La Méndez doing? Is she still
Alive?

Johnny.   And well off, living in Granada.

Chiquiznaque.   The poor chap's still in love with her!

Escarramán.   What do

They say of me at home since bad luck's
Kept me overseas?

Straybird.   A million things:
You've been gibbeted by actors on
The stage.

Wagtail.   The kids grind up your bones and marrow
In a stew of speculations.

Preener.   You've
Become their god. What more can you want?

Chiquiznaque.   In every street and square they sing
    about you.
In every house, at all the shows, they dance
The Escarramán. You've given poets more
To do than Troy gave Vergil.

Johnny.   They shout your name
In stables.

Preener.   You're curried with the horses by
The grooms. And washerwomen ring your name out
On the riverbanks.

Chiquiznaque.   Cloth shearers slice
You with their shears. You're much more famous than
The old gray mare.

Straybird.   They discuss your floggings
In the Indies. In Rome they weep about
Your tribulations. Dancing housemaids wear
Their buskins out ad infinitum.

Vademecum.   Good Lord,
They've pounded you like privet and plucked you
Like flowers, pealed out your name like church bells till
It's commoner than schoolboys sniveling at
Their catechism. Among the gilded youth,
Some other dances almost rival yours,
But in the end it's yours that takes first place.

Escarramán.   Tear me to bits, but give me fame. To leave
My mark I'd burn the Ephesian Temple down.

*The Musicians suddenly begin to play and sing this
ballad:*

> Now when brave Escarramán
> Broke out with his galley chains,
> Weren't the police surprised!
> Freed himself by taking pains!

Escarramán.   Is that a toast to me, by any chance?
You think that I've forgotten how to dance?
Well, I am lighter on my feet than ever.
I'll show you: strike it up—and both together!

Wagtail.   Oh, he's the best I've seen of any dancer,
Look how neat his steps are!

Vademecum.   Quick and clever.

Johnny.   That's just the touch to give Trampagos'
Wedding.

Escarramán.   Go on and play. I'll shake like mercury.

Musician.   Follow me as I sing; you can't go wrong.

Escarramán.   Then play! I'm raring to outdo myself.

Preener.   I'm mad to see him do it.

Musician.   Ready?

Chiquiznaque.   Play.

The Musicians sing:

> Now when brave Escarramán
> Broke out with his galley chains,
> Weren't the police surprised!
> Freed himself by taking pains!
> Now he's back to show the world
> How to dance with skill and cunning,
> Nimbleness of toe and heel,
> Royally as any king.
> Since our Coscolina's gone,
> Let the Preener take her place,
> Sweet as any orange blossom,
> Full of suppleness and grace.
> As the Wagtail clears her whistle,
> Starting up the promenade,
> Watch our great Escarramán
> Lead us in a galliard.

The galliard is played, and Escarramán dances it as a solo; at the end of a figure, the ballad continues:

> Let the Preener now begin
> Reeling out the low-down drag.
> She was first to show us how
> Properly to bump and sag.
> Now Escarramán will join her;
> Then the Wagtail follows you,
> Chiquiznaque and the Straybird.
> Johnny Brights, there, that's your cue.
> Look at that, they're perfect at it!
> Have you ever seen such sliding,
> Dipping, pacing, timing—no one
> Out of step—like sailboats gliding?
> Keep it up now, everyone.
> There's no other gang of pimps
> Nor a covey of such nymphs
> Anywhere in this wide world
> Like you, but it puffs and limps.
> What a wilderness of hands!
> How they fly, then lightly meet!
> What novel labyrinths are formed
> By their crisscrossing of feet!
> Change the step, just as you please.
> I can always play the tune.
> The Canary Walk or Gambol,
> Peasant Bread-and-Onion Swoon,
> Saraband or Sambapalo,
> I'm-So-Sorry-Dear and more.
> Good King Don Alfonso Crawl,
> Hoary in the days of old.

Escarramán. Play that old Canary Walk,
          I want to dance it all alone.

Musician. I'll smash the notes till they turn silver,
          Then your feet'll turn them gold.

The Canary Walk is played, and Escarramán dances it as a solo. Then, after the dance, he says:

Escarramán. Now let's have the Peasant Swoon,
          Bread-and-Onion in the chorus.
          Then the three of you can join me.

Musician.   St. John bless your twinkling toes.

*They dance the Peasant Swoon, which they know well,
and having finished it, Escarramán may ask for any
dance he wishes. When that's done, Trampagos says:*

Trampagos.   My wedding day is finer than
Any wedding day since Roland's.
Shout this with me to a man:
Long live great Escarramán!

All.   Long live great Escarramán!

CHOOSING A COUNCILMAN IN DAGANZO

(La Elección de los Alcaldes de Daganzo)

CAST

Cloven Hoof (Pesuña),
  college graduate

Peter Sneeze (Pedro
  Estornudo), clerk

Hardbread (Panduro),
  councilman

Alonso String Bean
  (Alonso Algarroba),
  councilman

Francis Gassing (Francisco
  de Humillos), peasant

John Craggy (Juan
  Berrocal), peasant

Michael Hock (Miguel
  Jarrete) peasant

Peter Frog (Pedro de la
  Rana), peasant

A Man

A Subsacristan

Gypsies, men and women

Musicians and Dancers

Choosing a Councilman in Daganzo

Enter Cloven Hoof, college graduate; Peter Sneeze, clerk; Hardbread and Alonso String Bean, councilmen.

Hardbread. Relax now. Take it easy. The good Lord willing,
Everything will be all right.

String Bean. But not
If we go on this way, at sixes and sevens.

Hardbread. Don't worry, I wouldn't be the least surprised
To see the whole thing settled soon, God willing.

String Bean. God willing, hell! It's settling this that counts.

Hardbread. String Bean, I see your tongue just slipped again!
Speak properly and respectfully.
I cannot say I like the way that sounds:
"God willing, hell!" Holy Pete, you're so
Damned set on being such a know-it-all,
You turn things topsy-turvy, willy-nilly.

String Bean. I'm a pureblood Christian from way back.
I'll have you know that I believe in God.

Cloven Hoof. That's fine. No one could ask for more.

String Bean. And if
I just said something wrong now, I admit it:
Yes, I'm a goose and take back all I said.

Sneeze. Enough. The good Lord asks for nothing more
Of the worst sinner but to live and to
Repent.

59

String Bean.   I'll say I live and I repent.
What's more, I know that God in Heaven can
Do what he wants, and nobody can stop
Him—when it rains especially.

Hardbread.   Rain falls
From clouds, not from God's Heaven, String Bean.

String Bean.   Saints alive! If all we've got to do
Here is to pick on one another, let's
Admit it. Then you'll see String Bean himself
Dig in and bite back for all he's worth.

Cloven Hoof.   *Redeamus ad rem*—stick to the point,
My dear String Bean and Hardbread. Don't
Waste precious time on foolish nonsense now—
Or did we come here just to start a squabble?
It never fails but that as soon as Hardbread
And String Bean get together, it's just as if
They kicked a thousand squalls and tempests up—
All on a thousand contradictory grounds.

Sneeze.   Cloven Hoof, the college man, is right.
Let's come to order and consider which
New councilman we'll choose now for next year,
And see to it that in Toledo they
Don't pick holes in him but say he's fit
For office. This is why we've come together.

Hardbread.   Here are four candidates for councilman:
John Craggy, Francis Gassing, Michael Hock,
And Peter Frog—all chaps with brains and good
Horse sense, and they're fit to judge not only in
Daganzo but also in Rome itself.

String Bean.   You mean
The town of Romanillos.

Sneeze.   More backbiting?
For Pete's sake, that's the limit now!

String Bean.   It's clear
Why he's called Sneeze: the clerk's got such a temper,
It blows up every time and hits his nose.
Don't worry, I won't say another word.

Hardbread.   Can there be any men on this whole plant—?

String Bean.   What *plant?* An eggplant? Just say *planet,*
　　My top-heavy friend, and you'll hit it right.

Hardbread.   I mean, in all the world you wouldn't find
　　Four men as brainy as our candidates.

String Bean.   Speaking for John Craggy, I know at least
　　He's got the sharpest sense——

Sneeze.　　　　　　　　　　Of what?

String Bean.　　　　　　　　　　　　Of taste.
　　He is a first-rate wine taster. At home
　　The other day he tapped a keg of mine
　　And said the clear wine smacked a bit of wood,
　　Of leather, and of iron. After I drained
　　The keg I found there lying at the bottom
　　A little stick, and fastened to it by
　　A leather thong there was a tiny key.

Sneeze.   Amazing! That's real skill! The man's a genius!
　　Someone like that, why, he could govern all
　　The wine towns—Alanís, Cazalla, even
　　Esquivias.

String Bean.   Take Michael Hock—a wizard!

Cloven Hoof.   How so?

String Bean.　　　　　　In shooting pellets from a crossbow.

Cloven Hoof.   What? Is he that good at it?

String Bean.　　　　　　　　　　　So good,
　　In fact, that if his shots did not always
　　Hit his own left hand, there wouldn't be
　　A bird left in the area.

Cloven Hoof.　　　　　A rare skill,
　　So necessary to a councilman.

String Bean.   What can I say of Francis Gassing? He
　　Can mend a shoe as good as any tailor.
　　And Peter Frog, he's got a memory
　　No one can beat. Now take that ballad on
　　The famous dog of Alba—why, he knows
　　Every single verse of it by heart.

Hardbread.   He gets my vote.

Sneeze.   Mine too.

String Bean.   I'll stick to Craggy.

Cloven Hoof.   No one gets mine till he can show more
　　Proof he's on the way to learning jurisprudence.

String Bean.   I have a good idea. It's this: just have
　　Each candidate come in and let good Master
　　Cloven Hoof, our college man, examine
　　Them; then, since he knows the law, we'll go
　　Along with him and that way see which one
　　Of them deserves to get the job.

Sneeze.   Great God,
　　But that's a very brilliant notion!

Hardbread.   I guess
　　His Jamesty could use the same idea
　　At court; just like they've got chef doctors,
　　We've got chef councilmen.

String Bean.   Hardbread, it's *chief*,
　　Not *chef*.

Hardbread.   You're the damnedest cricket anywhere!

String Bean.   It's *critic*, idiot!

Sneeze.   Ah, holy God,
　　But this String Bean's a petty monster!

String Bean.   My point
　　Is: just as barbers, blacksmiths, tailors, surgeons,
　　And the like must pass examinations,
　　So councilmen should be examined too.
　　Then anyone who's smart enough to pass
　　Would be awarded a diploma, and
　　With that he could support himself. With his
　　Diploma wrapped up nicely in a white
　　Tin tube, the beggar might just stumble on
　　A town one day where they would pay him well
　　For what he knows. Now almost always in
　　The villages these days, good councilmen
　　Are hard to find.

Cloven Hoof.   The point's well taken and

Well put. Now call in Craggy. Let him stand
Before us; then we'll see how deep and far
His knowledge ranges.

String Bean.   Frog, Gassing, Craggy,
Hock—all four candidates are here.

           Enter the four peasants.

                    And there
They stand before you.

Cloven Hoof.   Greetings, gentlemen.

Craggy.   Likewise, our best to you.

Hardbread.   Sit down. There
Are lots of chairs.

Gassing.   I'm so put out, I might
As well sit down.

Hock.   Praise be, we'll all sit down.

Frog.   Say, Gassing, what's put you out?

Gassing.   This naming of
A councilman—it just goes on and on.
By God, are we supposed to buy the job
With gifts—spring turkeys, jugs of honey, flocks
Of yearlings, and full wine sacks big enough
To wrap a steer in? If so, tell us, then
This way or that, we'll manage it somehow.

Cloven Hoof.   We don't want bribes here. What we're all
     agreed on
Is that the man best fitted for the job
Will so be called and chosen councilman.

Frog.   That's good. I'm satisfied.

Craggy.   Me too.

Cloven Hoof.   I'm glad.

Gassing.   I'll go along with that.

Hock.   And so will I.

Cloven Hoof.   Ready to be examined?

Gassing.   Get on with it.

Cloven Hoof.   All right, Gassing, tell me, can you read?

Gassing.   Of course not, and you wouldn't ever find
A relative of mine so mad he'd try
To learn the foolish stuff that sends men off
To the stake and women to the whorehouse.
No, I don't know how to read, but I
Know other things lots better than just reading.

Cloven Hoof.   What things are they?

Gassing.   I know my prayers by heart,
And pray them four or five times every week.

Frog.   You think that's all you need as councilman?

Gassing.   With that, and coming from the old pureblood
Christians, I'd dare to be a Roman senator.

Cloven Hoof.   All right, then. Now let Hock say what he
knows.

Hock.   I, Master Cloven Hoof, can read, though just
A bit. And I can spell, and I've been getting
Up my *ABC's* for three months now.
In five months more I hope to finish it.
Besides this knowledge I am studying,
I can shoe a plow up solid, brand
Four pairs of wild and bucking steers in just
About three hours. I'm in the best of health,
And I'm not deaf. I have no cataracts
Or coughing spells or rheumatism either.
I'm a good pureblood Christian like the rest
And shoot an arrow like a Cicero.

String Bean.   Those are rare talents in a councilman,
So varied and so necessary!

Cloven Hoof.   Next.
And what does Craggy know?

Craggy.   Upon my tongue
Lies all I know, and in my throat. No one
Alive can beat me as a wine taster.
Stamped on my palate are the tastes of sixty-
Six wines, all different.

String Bean.   So you want

To be a councilman?

Craggy.   Want and need
 To be. Once I've been tanked with Bacchus, all
 My senses slide together, and when that happens
 I feel that I could give Lycurgus lessons
 In the law, and wipe myself with Solon.

Hardbread.   Be careful now, we're at a council meeting!

Craggy.   I'm not a prude and not a pig, but all
 I have to say is—serve me right, don't mess
 Me up, or else I'll break this joint apart!

Cloven Hoof.   Who are you threatening here? I tell you,
    Master
 Craggy, that won't get you anywhere.
 Now what does Peter Frog know?

Frog.   As my name
 Is Frog, I don't sing well. And so, instead
 Of boasting of my brains, I'll state what I
 Believe. Gentlemen, if I, by chance,
 Were chosen councilman, I wouldn't use
 As light a staff of office as is usual.
 I'd make mine out of solid oak, two inches
 Thick, for fear the weight of any purse
 Of ducats all too pleasantly would bend it—
 Not to mention other gifts, those favors,
 Promises, and pledges, heavy as lead,
 And all unfelt until they crush your ribs,
 Body and soul. Also, with this in mind,
 I'd be courteous and civil, stern
 At times, but not inflexible. I'd not
 Insult the wretch whose crimes bring him before me.
 A cutting word that's meanly spoken by
 A judge can do more damage than the sentence,
 However cruel it is. Power should
 Not stifle courtesy, nor should the offender
 In his subjection make a judge act proud
 And overbearing.

String Bean.   Listen, by God, our Frog
 Here sings more sweetly than a dying swan!

Hardbread.   His speech was full of censorful ideas.

String Bean.   Meaning the Censor Cato, as Master
Hardbread, our councilman, did not quite say.

Hardbread.   That's it,
Criticize me!

String Bean.   In good time, I will.

Sneeze.   Now don't do it again. String Bean, you have
A mean fault-finding streak in you!

String Bean.   Oh, that's
Enough—you scribe!

Sneeze.   Scribe, is it? You Pharisee!

Cloven Hoof.   Holy Peter, all this stuff outrages
Rage.

String Bean.   I was joking.

Sneeze.   So was I.

Cloven Hoof.   Then once and for all, let's stop it.

String Bean.   Well, once a liar,
Always a liar.

Sneeze.   And whoever tells
The truth speaks truly.

String Bean.   True.

Sneeze.   Then there you are.
Period.

Gassing.   Now Frog's ideas are neither
Here nor there. Just let him get his fist
Around the staff of office, then see if he
Won't change into a different man from what
He seems right now.

Cloven Hoof.   There's something in what Gassing
Says.

Gassing.   And I'll say more: give me that staff,
I'll never waver, change, or alter once.

Cloven Hoof.   Well, here's the staff. You may regard
Yourself a councilman right now.

String Bean.   Of all things! Isn't
 That a left-handed staff you're giving him?

Gassing.   What do you mean, left-handed?

String Bean.   Well, it is
 Left-handed, isn't it? Even a deaf-mute
 Could see it is, standing a mile away.

Gassing.   Then how can you expect me to judge right
 When the staff you give me is left-handed?

Sneeze.   The devil's gotten into String Bean. Now who
 Ever heard of a left-handed staff?

A Man comes in.

Man.   Gentlemen, there are some Gypsies here,
 And some exquisite Gypsy girls. And though
 We said Your Honors are in conference, they still
 Insist on coming in to entertain you.

Cloven Hoof.   Let them in. We'll see if we can use
 Them at the Corpus Christi festival.
 That's under my direction.

Hardbread.   They're very welcome.

Craggy.   Have them come in at once.

Gassing.   I'm for it too.

Hock.   And I'll vote yes.

Frog.   They're Gypsies, aren't they?
 Watch out, they'll lift the noses off your faces.

Man.   They aren't waiting to be called; they're here.

*Enter the Gypsy Musicians and two Gypsy girls,
 brilliantly dressed. The girls dance when the Musicians
 strike up and sing the following ballad:*

Musicians.   We bring greetings from our tribe
         To Daganzo's councilmen,
         Good and brave in all you do,
         Upright, noblehearted men.
         Canny men you are who choose
         One best suited for the place
         Out of all the candidates,

           Disregarding faith or race.
           It appears that Heaven made you
           (Starry heaven's what we mean):
           Samsons all in what you know,
           Solons all in might and main.

Hock.   Their song is full of history!

Gassing.   Those girls
  And chaps are wonderful—so spare, so slender!

String Bean.   I say they're sort of gross and fat.

Cloven Hoof.   Silence!

Musicians. As the winds must shift and veer,
           As the trees must change attire,
           Threadbare, naked through the winter,
           Decked in leaves through summertime,
           So our dances change in time,
           Step by step, measure for measure;
           As you know, it's women's pleasure
           To be as fickle as the weather.

  Hail, Daganzo's councilmen, live long;
  Be straight as palm trees and like oak trees strong.

               They dance.

Hock. By God, that song's well sung.

Gassing.   With feeling, too.

Craggy. Those are words that should be printed; they'll
  Preserve our memory forever and
  A day. Amen.

Cloven Hoof. Now be still, won't you?

Musicians.   Live on and live forever,
            And, as night succeeds
            Each day, let centuries
            Pass swiftly by but never
            Change you, while you stay
            At thirty years of age.
            May no leaves ever wither
            On your sturdy trees,
            And may the winds that rise

> And drown men in their gales
> Become a gentle breeze
> Lapping on your shoals.

Hail, Draganzo's councilmen, live long;
Be straight as palm trees and like oak trees strong.

Cloven Hoof. I can't say much for that refrain, and yet
The song's not altogether bad.

Craggy.   Hey, quiet.

Musicians.   I'll stamp this dust
                    Until I bust.
                    I'll make it bust
                    Until I'm dust.

Hardbread. Listen to those musicians! They're making
Mincemeat of the song.

Gassing.   They're devils—those Gypsies!

Musicians.   Hard as rock
                    Though it may be,
                    I'll stamp the ground
                    So heavily,
                    Love will break
                    Open for me
                    My own grave
                    Underground.
                    Love has crushed
                    All my luck
                    In the dust
                    So deep and quick
                    I must kick
                    The hardest ground
                    To bedevil
                    All the evil
                    I distrust,
                    Dead and silent
                    Underground.
                    Happiness
                    Has passed me by,
                    Leaving only
                    This small dust.

Enter a Subsacristan, looking terribly distraught.

Subsacristan.　Holy blazes, master councilmen,
You carry on like rowdies—it's disgraceful!
Heavens, is this the way you govern our
Town—with dancing girls, guitars, and revels?

Cloven Hoof.　Grab him, Hock.

Hock.　　　　　　　　　　　　I've got him.

Cloven Hoof.　　　　　　　　　Now get a blanket.
Good God, this rascal here deserves a tossing.
The impudent damn fool—the nerve of him!

Subsacristan.　Listen, gentlemen!

String Bean.　　　　　　　　　I'll get the blanket,
I'm off like the wind.

　　　　　　　　　　　　　　　　Exit String Bean.

Subsacristan.　　　　　　Watch out, I warn you! I'm
A priest.

Cloven Hoof.　You, a priest? Oh, you scoundrel!

Subsacristan.　I am a priest—well, anyway, I've got
My tonsure; that's as good as being one.

Hardbread.　We'll see about that, said the grackle bird.

Subsacristan.　Grackle bird? Not here.

Hardbread.　　　　　　　　　　Oh, there'll soon
Be grackles here to peck your tongue and eyes out.

Frog.　Tell me, poor wretch: what demon got your tongue?
Who sent you here to damn authority?
Is it your job to rule the commonwealth?
Stick to your own affairs; stick to your bells.
Leave governing to those who know something
About it: they're better at it than we are.
And if they do it badly, pray that they'll
Improve; if well, pray God to keep them with us.

Cloven Hoof.　Our Frog's a saint, and he's been blessed
with brains.

　　　　Enter String Bean, returning with the blanket.

String Bean.   You can't say now we didn't have a blanket!

Cloven Hoof.   Take hold, everyone—including Gypsies.
   Now up with him, my friends!

Subsacristan.   Help! They'll do it,
   Too. By God, don't get me angry or you'll
   Find out I won't stand for any nonsense.
   Holy Peter, if you touch one hair
   On my blanket, you're excommunicated!

Frog.   No more, that'll do for him. The poor chap's
   Been punished; he's sorry now and should repent.

Subsacristan.   What's worse, I'm sore all over. From
   Now on, I'm dumb. I'll stitch my lips with cobbler's
   Twine.

Frog.   That's the idea.

Cloven Hoof.   Gypsies, come home with me,
   I've something to discuss.

Gypsies.   We're right behind you.

Cloven Hoof.   Election postponed until tomorrow, when,
   I tell you now, I'll vote for Peter Frog.

Gypsies.   What shall we chant, sir?

Cloven Hoof.   Anything you like.

Hardbread.   There's no one better than our Frog at
   chanting.

Hock.   Not only chanting, but enchanting too.

   Exeunt singing, "I'll stamp this dust . . ."

THE HAWK-EYED SENTINEL

(La Guarda Cuidadosa)

CAST

Soldier

Lorenzo Aisles (Lorenzo Pasillas), subsacristan

Boy (Andrew), begging alms

Boy (Manuel), selling ribbons, etc.

Cristina, scullery maid

Her Master

Her Mistress

Shoemaker

Grackles (Grajales), sacristan

Musicians

The Hawk-Eyed Sentinel

Enter a shabby Soldier with a very worn sash and a spyglass, and behind him a mean-looking Sacristan.

Soldier. What do you want of me, bodiless spirit?

Sacristan. Who's a spirit? I'm real flesh and blood.

Soldier. Well, all the same, on the authority of my hard luck, I order you to tell me who you are and what you're looking for down this street.

Sacristan. My answer to that is, on the authority of my good luck, I'm Lorenzo Aisles, subsacristan of this parish, and I'm here to find what I'm looking for while you're here looking for what you won't find.

Soldier. Are you by any chance looking for Cristina, the scullery maid in this house?

Sacristan. *Tu dixisti.* You said it.

Soldier. Then look here, you blasted joker!

Sacristan. I'm looking, you heretical jack!

Soldier. All right, then, jack, ace, and queen—if it's all a game of cards to you. Now all I need's three kings and another jack for the full house that takes the first pot here. I say it again: look here. Don't you get it yet, Mr. Aisles, that just as sure as my pike will run an aisle through you, Cristina is *my* sweetheart?

Sacristan. And don't you get it, you bedraggled octopus, that she's *mine,* pledged wholly and solely to me, the highest bidder?

Soldier. By God, I'll cut you to shreds and dice up your skull!

Sacristan. Never mind me and my skull. Those shredded stockings and that diced-up tunic of yours should keep you happy awhile.

Soldier. Have you spoken with Cristina often?

Sacristan. Whenever I please.

Soldier. Did you give her any gifts?

Sacristan. A good many.

Soldier. How many, and what sort of thing?

Sacristan. Oh, I gave her one of those huge quince boxes, packed with holy-wafer crumbs, white as driven snow, and to top it off, four wax-candle stubs, whiter than ermine.

Soldier. What else did you give her?

Sacristan. A thousand sweet nothings wrapped in a *billet doux.*

Soldier. And she—what was her answer to that?

Sacristan. A thousand cozy little signs of soon becoming my wife.

Soldier. But aren't you sworn to celibacy?

Sacristan. Not at all. I'm a lay brother and can marry when and whomever I please, as you'll soon find out.

Soldier. Come here, you short-cropped rascal, and answer this one. If the girl's been so nice to you (which I don't believe) because of your wretched little gifts, what won't she say to the munificence of mine? Just the other day, I sent her a love letter written on nothing less than the reverse side of a petition to His Majesty, where I'd listed the merits of my past services to the Crown and outlined my immediate needs—since the soldier who says he's poor needn't be ashamed of it. The petition was approved and returned to me for the Chief Almsgiver, and though the document's worth at least four to six *reales,* an impulse of unparalleled generosity and conspicuous nonchalance led me to write my love letter, as I say, on the reverse side. And I know it left my sinful hands only to find its way to her almost sainted ones.

Sacristan. Didn't you send her anything else?

Soldier. Sighs, tears, sobs, paroxysms, fainting fits, and that whole flock of devices good lovers have to use to show their feelings on every occasion.

Sacristan. Did you serenade her?

Soldier. With my griefs and sorrows, my burning hopes and my despair.

Sacristan. Oh well, as for me, I time the ringing of my bells to every step she takes; in fact, the din has put the whole neighborhood up in arms, and just because I want to make her happy and let her know I'm up in that belfry ringing out my devotions to her. And when I should be tolling for the dead, my bells peal out a sort of call to vespers, though solemnly, of course.

Soldier. It's there you have the upper hand. I've got nothing to ring—not for love or money.

Sacristan. Then how does Cristina take to all the great things you've done for her?

Soldier. By never seeing me or speaking to me; by cursing me every time we meet on the street; by dumping her dirty wash water over me and then her dirty dishwater. And that's every day, because I come here every day to stand guard at her door, because I'm her hawk-eyed sentinel, and because I'm her dog in the manger, and so forth. I don't possess her, but neither will anyone else while I'm alive. And that's why you'd better move on now, Mr. Subsacristan, since it's only my respect for your holy order that keeps me from smashing your skull to bits.

Sacristan. You'd have to do a lot of smashing to make anything look as smashed as those clothes of yours.

Soldier. Clothes don't make the man. A soldier in tattered battle dress is as honorable as the college man in a worn gown that shows how long he's studied. Move on now, or I'll do just what I promised.

Sacristan. Is that because you see I'm unarmed? Well, just you wait here, Mr. Hawk-Eyed Sentinel, and you'll see the wide swathe I'll cut through you.

Soldier. You, you narrow little Aisle? Never!

Sacristan. You wait and see—said the tortoise to the hare.

Exit Sacristan.

Soldier. Ah, women, women! They're all—or almost all —so fickle and capricious. How, Cristina, can you spurn this flower, this garden of soldierly virtue, to wallow in that dung pile of a subsacristan, you who could at least have a full-fledged sacristan or even a canon of the Church? But I'll see that no good comes of it; I'll do everything to spoil your little game. I'll keep my eye peeled here at your door for anyone who even only imagines becoming your lover. And that way I'll earn the name of hawk-eyed sentinel.

Enter a Boy with his box and wearing a green smock, in the manner of those who beg alms for a holy image.

Boy. Alms, alms, in God's name, for a lamp of oil for our lady Saint Lucy, to protect your eyesight. Anybody home? Any alms today?

Soldier. One minute there, Saint Lucy boy—come here. Just what do you want at this house?

Boy. Don't you see, sir? Alms for a lamp of oil for our lady Saint Lucy.

Soldier. Is it alms for the lamp or for the oil you're begging? Because if you say alms for the lamp of oil, it's like the lamp belonged to the oil and not the oil to the lamp.

Boy. Anyone would know it's oil for the lamp and not a lamp for the oil I'm begging.

Soldier. And so you get alms at this house?

Boy. Two coppers a day.

Soldier. And who comes out to give them to you?

Boy. Whoever happens to be around, though usually it's that little scullery maid Cristina—pretty as a picture, fine as gold!

Soldier. Oh, so the maid's fine and pretty, is she?

Boy. Yes, or like a string of pearls.

Soldier. So she's not so bad, is she?

Boy. I could be made of stone, and still I'd like her looks.

Soldier. What's your name? I don't want to be calling you Saint Lucy again.

Boy. My name is Andrew, sir.

Soldier. See here, little Andrew, this is what I've got to tell you: you take these eight coppers and consider you've been paid four days' worth at this house, where you usually get them from Cristina. And now, off with you —and remember, I don't want to see hide nor hair of you at this door, even to borrow a light, in the next four days, or I'll kick your ribs in.

Boy. I won't even be back this month—if I happen to think of it. Don't get angry, sir, I'm going.

> *Exit Boy.*

Soldier. Well, hawk-eyed sentinel, don't you be caught napping!

> *Enter another Boy, calling out his wares.*

Boy. Who'll buy my hair ribbons, Flemish lace, Cambrai linen, Portuguese yarn?

> *Cristina, at the window.*

Cristina. Say, Manuel! Do you have any piping for some shirts?

Boy. Indeed I do—and very good stuff too.

Cristina. Then come up. My mistress wants some.

Soldier. O falling star, ruination! Hope, my guiding star, now disappears! You there, Hair Ribbons, or whatever your name is—do you know that girl who just called you from the window?

Boy. Yes, of course. But why do you ask, sir?

Soldier. She's sweet, she's attractive—isn't she?

Boy. Yes, *I* think so.

Soldier. Well, what *I* think is—you're not going inside that house. And if you dare, by God, I'll grind your bones up, one by one.

Boy. You mean I can't go in when people want my stuff?

Soldier. Get along with you. Don't answer back! I'll let you have it, as I said I would, and right away!

Boy. What a nasty business! Easy now, Soldier, I'm going.

                                            Exit Manuel.
                    Cristina, at the window.

Cristina. Are you coming in, Manuel?

Soldier. Manuel is gone, O lovely lady of the lively shirt pipings—or I might say, lady of the living and the dead, since you hold sway over both.

Cristina. What a disgusting brute you are! What are you doing on this street, hanging on that door?

                                            Exit Cristina.

Soldier. My sunlight's gone behind a cloud.

Enter a Shoemaker with a pair of brand-new little slippers in his hand, and as he is about to enter the house the Soldier stops him.

Soldier. Are you looking for anyone inside that house, my good fellow?

Shoemaker. Yes, I'm looking for someone.

Soldier. And for whom, if it isn't too much to ask?

Shoemaker. Not at all. I'm looking for the scullery maid who lives inside, and I'm delivering these slippers she asked me to make for her.

Soldier. Meaning, sir, that you're her shoemaker?

Shoemaker. I've often fitted her with shoes.

Soldier. And now you're going to have her try on those slippers?

Shoemaker. No, that's not necessary. If they were boots with heels, like those she usually wears, then she'd have to try them on.

Soldier. And these, are they paid for or not?

Shoemaker. No, but she'll pay me now.

Soldier. Sir, would you do me a tremendous favor and let me have these slippers on credit? I'll give you security of equal value till the day after tomorrow, when I expect to have a lot of money.

Shoemaker. Yes, of course. But let's have the pledge. I'm only a poor artisan and can't afford to trust anybody.

Soldier. Sir, I'll give you a toothpick I especially prize. It's easily worth over a crown. Now, where is your shop, sir, so I can redeem this pledge later?

Shoemaker. On the main square, in the portico near one of the pillars, and the name is Juan Juncos.

Soldier. Well, sir, here's my toothpick. Cherish it, please, since it belongs to me.

Shoemaker. What! Just a cheap little wooden sliver that's not worth two cents—and you expect me to cherish it?

Soldier. Me oh my! I'm giving it to you only to remind myself. When I put this hand in my pocket and find the toothpick gone, I immediately recall that you, sir, have it, and so I go at once to redeem it. Yes, sir, on my honor as a soldier, that's the only reason. But if that's not enough, I'll throw in my sash and my spyglass. A man who's flush doesn't niggle over securities.

Shoemaker. I may only be a shoemaker, but yet I'm not so crude as to strip you of your prize possessions. So keep them, please, and I'll keep my slippers, which mean something to me too.

Soldier. What size are they?

Shoemaker. Barely five.

Soldier. My purse is even barer, dearest slippers. I haven't the money to pay for you, dear slippers. Master Shoemaker, listen to me. I'll compose a poem on the spot. It's just come into my head and scans perfectly: "Slippers of My Heart."

Shoemaker. Are you a poet, sir?

Soldier. One of the best, as you'll see. Listen carefully. "Slippers of My Heart":

> Ah, love is such a cruel tyrant
> That, heedless of the faith I keep
> (Vainly in my heart compliant),
> Makes slippers, where her toes will sleep,
> Slap me down and act defiant.
>
> By this feat and other feats,
> O slippers shy, O slippers neat,
> Intended for Cristina's feet,
> You have become (my soul repeats)
> The slippers stamping out my heart . . . beat.

Shoemaker. I don't know much about poetry, but yours sounds good to me, like Lope's—that's to say, like all poetry that's any good, or is supposed to be.

Soldier. Well, sir, since I can't make you give me the slippers on credit (little as it comes to, especially for "such sweet treasures, to my grief discovered"), at least keep them for two days till I call for them. But meanwhile, I tell you, my dear shoemaker, don't try to see Cristina or breathe a word to her about this.

Shoemaker. I'll do as you say, Soldier, because it's clear that the two feet that carry you are poverty and suspicion.

Soldier. You're no shoemaker—you're a college wit!

Shoemaker. Ah, suspicion, suspicion, leads to perdition.

Exit Shoemaker.

Soldier. There, you see? If you didn't watch seriously, like a hawk-eyed sentinel, all those flies would go swarming into the cellar where the precious wine of your bliss is stored. But whose voice is that? Can it be hers, my lovely Cristina's, cheering herself up as she sweeps the floors or washes the dishes?

Amid the sounds of dishes being washed within, this song is heard:

> My love I entwine,
> O sacristan mine!
> I'm yours forever,
> Sing hallelujah!

Soldier. Oh, that these ears of mine must listen to it! It's clear that sacristan's captured her heart. Ah, kitchen maid, the purest there is, was, or ever will be in the saintly calendar of maids! Why, as you wash the Talaveran crockery with your hands and polish it up till it glitters and shines like silver, why not scrub out of your heart those vile subsacrisatanic devotions?

Enter Cristina's Master.

Master. Young man, what is it you're wanting or expecting, standing in front of this house?

Soldier. I want more than is good for me and expect more than I'll get. But who are you, sir, to ask?

Master. I own this house.

Soldier. Cristina's master?

Master. Exactly.

Soldier. Sir, please come closer and glance at this roll of papers. Contained in this spyglass is the story of my military career: twenty-two certificates signed by twenty-two generals under whose banners I served, not to mention thirty-four others signed by as many field marshals, who deigned to honor me.

Master. As far as I know, there never were so many Spanish generals or field marshals in a hundred years of military action.

Soldier. Sir, you are a peaceful citizen, with no reason to trouble your head over military matters. But let your eyes scan these documents and you'll find all their names, one after the other, just as I said.

Master. I take your word for it. But why should all this affect me?

Soldier. Simply because these papers confirm what I'm about to tell you, namely: that I am being considered for the post of commandant at one of the three armed fortresses in the Kingdom of Naples—meaning, of course, Gaeta, Barletta, and Reggio.

Master. So far, nothing you've said concerns me in the least.

Soldier. Yet I know it must, God willing.

Master. In what way?

Soldier. Because unless Heaven itself collapses, I'll be commandant at one of the three fortresses, and I want to marry Cristina now. When I'm her husband, you, sir, will be able to use me and my considerable holdings as your own; for I won't begrudge the kind treatment that my dearly beloved consort has received at your hands. I am touched by it.

Master. Sir, you must be touched in the head.

Soldier. So, Mr. Sweetmeat, you still don't see how much this concerns you. Well, unless you surrender the girl to me right now, you won't set foot in that doorway.

Master. What sort of nonsense is this? Who'd have the gall to keep me from walking into my own house?

Enter Subsacristan Aisles, armed with a pot lid and a rusty sword; Sacristan Grackles accompanies him, wearing a helmet and holding a yardstick or pole, with a foxtail tied to the end of it.

Sacristan. There he is, Grackles, that's the fly in my ointment!

Grackles. It's too bad these weapons are so flimsy, because with one blow I'd hurl him to kingdom come.

Master. Hold on now, gentlemen! Are you mad? Are you out for murder?

Soldier. Scoundrels! So there's a gang of you now, you fiends, you pseudosacristans! I swear I'll run you through, though you've taken more orders than a college of cardinals. Cowards! Threaten me with a foxtail, will you? What do you think I am, a drunkard? Or one of your plaster saints that needs dusting?

Grackles. Oh, you're just a fly around a wine jar I've got to brush away.

Cristina and her Mistress at the window.

Cristina. Madam, madam, look: they're murdering my master! I see more than two thousand swords raised against him! Oh, the glitter is blinding!

Mistress. It's true, my dear. God preserve him! Saint Ursula protect him with her eleven thousand virgins! Come, Cristina, let us go down and help him if we can.

Master. Holy Heaven, gentlemen, control yourselves. You should know it's not fair fighting two against one!

Soldier. Stand back, foxtail, and stand back, you little pot lid. Don't stir me up, because if you do, I'll kill and eat the two of you, then toss your bones two miles out the back door of Hell!

Master. Stop it now, I tell you. If you don't, by God, I'll forget myself, and one of you will pay dearly for this!

Soldier. Me, I'll stop—out of respect for that divine image living in your house.

Sacristan. That image won't do you any good now, even if she worked miracles.

Soldier. The guts of this rogue, to come swishing at me with a foxtail! At me, who never blinked an eye when cannons outboomed the heaviest gun in Lisbon!

Enter Cristina and her Mistress.

Mistress. Oh, my dear husband! Have they hurt you any, sweetheart?

Cristina. Oh, sweet Jesus! It's my sacristan and my soldier brawling!

Soldier. Notice she said *my soldier,* though I have to share the *my* with that sacristan.

Master. I'm not hurt, my dear, but you should know that all this fighting is over Cristina.

Mistress. Over Cristina, you say?

Master. As far as I can make out, these fellows are madly jealous over her.

Mistress. Girl, is this true?

Cristina. Yes, madam.

Mistress. See how shamelessly she admits it! Has one of them dishonored you?

Cristina. Yes, madam.

Mistress. Which one?

Cristina. The sacristan dishonored me the other day when I went to market.

Mistress. How many times have I told you, sir, that this girl is not to be let out of the house? Now that she's grown up, it's not proper to let her out of our sight. What will her father say, who left her spick-and-span in our protection? And where, hussy, did he take you to dishonor you?

Cristina. Nowhere—just there, in the middle of the street.

Mistress. What's that? In the middle of the street?

Cristina. Yes, on Toledo Street, in the sight of God and the whole world, he called me dirty, brazen, shameless, and indecent—and other bad names like that. And all because he's jealous of that soldier.

Master. So there's nothing more between you than those insults on the street?

Cristina. Certainly not, because then he got over his anger.

Mistress.   Ah, now I can breathe again! I almost thought she was beyond redemption!

Cristina.   Besides, everything else he said was written down in this pledge he gave me—the promise to be my husband; and I've kept it here like gold wrapped in a cloth.

Master.   Give it here. Let's see it.

Mistress.   Will you read it aloud, husband?

Master.   It goes this way: "I, Lorenzo Aisles, subsacristan of this parish, do hereby subscribe that I dearly love (most dearly, indeed) Mistress Cristina de Parraza and in token of this pledge do give her this document, signed by my name, dated in Madrid, in the parish of St. Andrew, the sixth of May, of the present year, one thousand six hundred and eleven. Witnesses: my heart and my three faculties of mind: understanding, will, and memory. Lorenzo Aisles." An odd way of engaging to be married!

Sacristan.   Included in what I say about loving her dearly is everything she may wish me to do for her, because once you pledge your good will, you pledge everything.

Master.   Well, then, you'd really marry her if she agreed?

Sacristan.   With all my heart, though I lose the hope of eleven pieces of eight in annuity to go toward a chaplaincy, which my grandmother in a recent letter from home said she would settle on me if I remained a bachelor.

Soldier.   If good will is going to count for anything here, it's now thirty-nine days since I gave Cristina my word at the Segovia Bridge. And that includes my three faculties of mind too. And if she wishes to be my wife, it should also be added that there's a difference between a commandant of a famous fortress and an incomplete, half-pint sacristan, who even falls short of the half.

Master.   Do you want to get married, Cristina?

Cristina.   Yes, I do.

Master. Then choose the one you like better from these two who proposed.

Cristina. I'm embarrassed.

Master. Don't be. Marrying, like eating, is a matter of personal taste: we choose to please ourselves and not somebody else.

Cristina. Thank you, sir, and you too, madam, who've brought me up and would know the husband best suited to me, though I'd still like to choose one myself.

Soldier. Cast your eye upon me, lass. Observe the elegant figure, soldier that I am, commandant to be. Consider my vigor and my spirit—the most gallant man alive. By the thread of this poor garment, you may unwind the skein of my gentility.

Sacristan. In me you get a musician, Cristina, though only at church bells. In decorating a tomb or fixing up the church for solemn holidays, there's not a better sacristan anywhere. And I can still perform those jobs after I'm married, and make a princely living at it.
Master. Very well, my child. Now choose the one you like. I shall like him too, and that way you'll end the quarrel between these two tremendous rivals.

Soldier. I agree to it.

Sacristan. And I give myself over to it.

Cristina. I choose the sacristan.

Enter the Musicians.

Master. Then bring on those fellows who work for my neighbor the barber. With their voices and guitars they'll help us celebrate the engagement, singing and dancing. And the soldier will be my guest.

Soldier. I accept, for

> *In a fight where might makes right,*
> *Losers can't be choosers. Quite.*

Musician. So we've come in time. We'll use those words as our refrain.

The refrain is sung.

Soldier. A woman's choice will always fall
On men who've got no sense at all.
Her taste is bad, and oh, how sad
That she despises men of worth
And thinks the mud is solid earth.
How could she know what courage is
Whom only wealth encourages?
She'll let a manly soldier down
And grab a pipsqueak sacristan.
I'm not surprised; who but a fool
Would think because he's found a hole
In church, he's holy—safe inside,
Where only criminals would hide?

In a fight where might makes right,
Losers can't be choosers. Quite.

Sacristan. All the battles that a soldier
Boasts of only mean he's older.
Once he deserts his regiment,
Without a cent to pay his rent,
He's got to play the conquering hero,
Full of bluster, brag, and beer, oh!—
And lose, because he's such a bully,
What I gain by working coolly.
I'm not insulted by your notions.
I won, now go and have conniptions.
Sore losers live inside a cage,
Where all they do is rant and rage.

In a fight where might makes right,
Losers can't be choosers. Quite.

They all exit, singing and dancing.

THE
BASQUE
IMPOSTOR

(El Vizcaíno Fingido)

CAST

Solórzano

Quiñones

Doña Cristina

Doña Brígida

A Silversmith

Two Musicians

A Constable

The Basque Impostor

Enter Solórzano and Quiñones.

Solórzano. Here are the purses. Now, to all appearances, they're exactly alike, including the two chains inside them. All you have to do is help me with my plan. And shrewd as she is, this time we'll really fix that Sevillian wench.

Quiñones. What sort of honor or skill is there in cheating a woman that you take such great pains to do it?

Solórzano. It's fun tricking that kind of woman. Besides, I'm not carrying the joke too far. I mean, I won't offend God or hurt the woman herself. A joke's not funny if it makes a person look contemptible.

Quiñones. Fair enough. I'll do as you wish and help in every way you say, since I'm as good a fraud as you are, and that's no small praise. Where are you off to now?

Solórzano. Straight to the wench's house. Now, don't wander off from here. I'll call for you when it's time.

Quiñones. I'll be waiting, rooted to this spot.

Exeunt both of them.

Enter Doña Cristina and Doña Brígida: Cristina without a shawl and Brígida wearing one, excited and very frightened.

Cristina. Good Lord! What's wrong, Brígida my pet? You look like you're ready to give up the ghost.

Brígida. Cristina dear, fan my brow, dampen my face

with some water, I'm dying, I'm done for—it's torn the heart clean out of me! God help me! Quick, call a priest!

Cristina. What's the matter? Oh, this is awful! Pet, won't you tell me what's happened? Have you seen a ghost? Is it bad news? Did your mother die? Has your husband come back? Were your jewels stolen?

Brígida. No, I haven't seen a ghost, my mother's not dead, and my husband's not due back yet—he has three months more to finish his business abroad—and nobody's stolen my jewels. But something much worse has happened.

Cristina. Come, tell me, Brígida my pet. Don't keep me waiting; I'll be shaking like a leaf till I know what it's all about.

Brígida. Well, darling, part of this nasty business concerns you too. Do wipe my face—I'm bathed all over in a cold sweat. What we poor women of the streets have to put up with! Just when we manage to hold up our heads a bit after all the scrounging around we must do here and there, somebody comes along to nip us in the bud!

Cristina. For heaven's sake, pet, come to the point. Tell me what's happened to you and what this nasty business is that concerns me too.

Brígida. I'll say it concerns you! And especially if you're sensible, as I know you are. You must be told about this, my dear. Coming this way to see you, I was passing the Guadalajara Gate, where throngs of people and policemen were gathered around a crier, and the announcement was that from now on, no carriages or women with veils are permitted in the streets.

Cristina. And that's all your bad news?

Brígida. Well, could there be anything worse for the likes of us?

Cristina. I imagine, my pet, it's just some newfangled notion about using carriages. Surely no one's thinking of doing away with them completely. But that wouldn't be

such a bad thing either, for I've heard tell that horseback riding in Spain has fallen off terribly, when ten to a
dozen young blades stuff themselves into a carriage and
go whipping around the streets day and night, as though
the existence of mounts and horsemen had never in the
world entered their heads. So if they lose the pleasure of
knocking around in those landlocked galleys they call
carriages, they'll take to horseback again the way their
fathers did.

Brígida. Ah, Cristina, my dear! I also heard that a
few carriages will be permitted, but not if they're ridden
in or lent to women like—well, you know who I mean.

Cristina. That may do us all some good; for let me tell
you, pet, that military men are still arguing over which
is better, the cavalry or the infantry, and it's been shown
that our Spanish infantry is the world's best. So now it's
our duty, as daughters of joy, to show our elegance,
grace, and spirit when we walk. Besides, now that we'll
be going along with our faces plainly showing, none of
our men can say they've been cheated, since they'll be
getting a good look at us first.

Brígida. Oh, Cristina, don't say that! It was such fun
riding along perched in the rear of a carriage, moving
pretty as you please from one side to the other, and
showing your best face to anyone at all whenever you
liked. And believe me, so help me God, when I was riding in a borrowed carriage and thought how elegant I
looked inside, I swear I felt so proud that I really thought
myself a lady to the manner born and that a brace of
noblewomen might well be my servants.

Cristina. Well now, Brígida, don't you see how right
I am to say it's a good thing we're rid of the carriages, so
we can at least rid ourselves of the sin of pride? Besides, it wasn't fair to let a carriage put a counterfeit
lady on a par with a real one. Imagine the stranger who
clapped his eyes on a woman riding in a carriage, all
sparkling in her jewels and dressed to the teeth; the
courtesy he paid her would be wasted if he mistook her
for some grand lady. So that's why, my pet, you shouldn't
feel bad. But cheer up, brighten your smile, put on your

smart Sevillian silk shawl, and don't forget your new cork slippers with the silver straps, and sally forth down the streets. Why, I can tell you now, the flies will come swarming to the honeypot, if you want them around you. And if you work at it more than that, they'll come running to kiss you in your sleep.

Brígida. Bless you, darling. Your sweet advice has cheered me up. And what's more, I'll follow it. I'll spread the powder and the paint, show my face, and kick my heels a bit, with no one to bite my head off for doing it. For the fellow that people think is my husband isn't, though he's promised to marry me.

Cristina. Heavens! Who's this slipping so slyly into my house without knocking? Sir, what's your business here?

Enter Solórzano.

Solórzano. I trust you'll pardon my audacity, but opportunity makes the thief, you know. I found your door wide open, so I came in, excusing myself as I did so with the thought that I've come to serve you, not with words alone but with deeds. Now, if I may speak openly in the presence of this lady, I'll tell you what I've come for and why.

Cristina. To judge by your appearance, one would expect nothing but fine words and deeds. You may speak frankly, since Doña Brígida is such a close friend she's practically my second self.

Solórzano. With such assurance and your permission, I shall speak truthfully. Truly, then, madam, I am a courtier, but unknown to you.

Cristina. That's true enough.

Solórzano. And I've been hoping to serve you for some time now, having been struck by your beauty, your charming disposition, and superior manners. But straitened circumstances, I must say, have deterred me until now, when fate sent me from Biscay the son of a close friend of mine, a handsome young gentleman, a Basque, whom I was asked to take to Salamanca and to place there, through my good offices, among such respectable company as would instruct him in the finer graces. For, to tell you the truth, the young man's a bit dense, a little thick between the ears. Add to that handicap another, sad to say but sadder to possess, which is his somewhat more than usual weakness for wine. Mind you, it's not that he loses his head entirely, though he does, of course, get muddled. But when he's had a drop too much and he's four sheets to the wind, his generosity and joy are something to behold. He flings away everything he owns to anyone who asks for it—also, for that matter, to anyone who doesn't ask for it. Now, I propose, since all he has will be going to the devil anyway, to get some of it myself; and I could hit on nothing better than to bring him to your house (since he's so fond of women), shut him up inside here, and skin him like a cat. To begin with, I've brought you this chain in this purse. Measured by weight alone it's worth a hundred and twenty gold crowns. Take it, madam, and give me ten crowns now; I'll need that sum for certain expenses. Then if you add another twenty for supper tonight, I'll bring our donkey or little buffalo along (since I can lead him by the nose, as they say), and after one or two visits you can keep the chain, in exchange for which I ask nothing more than the ten crowns I need now. It's an excellent chain and of solid gold, not to mention the value of the workmanship. Here it is. You are welcome to it.

Cristina. I am much obliged to you, sir, for thinking of me in connection with so profitable an enterprise. But if I were to say what I feel, your generosity is so overwhelming that I'm confused and even a bit suspicious.

Solórzano. Suspicious of what, my dear lady?

Cristina. Of the fact that the chain might be a product of alchemy. For, as they say, all that glitters is not gold.

Solórzano. What you say makes very good sense. Not in vain are you known as the most prudent woman in the capital. And I am delighted to see how freely you open your heart to me, without mincing any words. But there's a way out of everything except death. If you would simply slip on your shawl or send someone you trust to see the silversmith, we'll have the chain weighed and assayed. And if it's as fine and precious as I say, you can let me have the ten crowns, entertain our little donkey, and end up by keeping the chain.

Cristina. There's a silversmith right here, only a few doors away; I know him well, and he'll easily clear up the question.

Solórzano. That's just what I want, what I love, and what I respect: God bless everything that's open and aboveboard.

Cristina. If you can trust me with the chain while I have it assayed, you may come back in a short while and I'll have the ten gold crowns for you.

Solórzano. Excellent! Madam, since I entrust you with my honor, how can I not entrust you with the chain? Have it assayed to your heart's content. I leave you now, to return in half an hour.

Cristina. Even sooner, if my neighbor is in.

Exit Solórzano.

Brígida. Cristina, darling, this is luck, and by the bucketful! Poor me, I'm so unlucky—I never bump into anyone who'd give me so much as a drink of water without my having to slave for it! Unless it's someone like that poet I ran into the other day on the street: full of the best sort of spirit and flourishing courtesy, he gives me a sonnet all about Pyramus and Thisbe, then offers to write three hundred more in my praise.

Cristina. You'd have been much better off finding a Genoese banker to give you three hundred *reales*.

Brígida. Well, naturally. I suppose those Genoese moneylenders are just aching to lend themselves out in the open and come to the hand like birds to seeds. Why, nowadays all they do is mope and look glum, with that decree hanging over them.

Cristina. Look, Brígida, here's something I know you can be sure of: one bankrupt Genoese is worth more than four solvent poets. Well, look who the good wind's blown in! It's my silversmith. Now, what can I do for you, my good neighbor? I declare, if I wasn't about to put on my shawl to go look for you.

Enter the Silversmith.

Silversmith. Please, Doña Cristina, you must do me a favor: try as hard as you can to get my wife to go to the play with you tomorrow. Because tomorrow afternoon I must be absolutely free of anyone hounding and tracking me down.

Cristina. I'll be delighted to do it. And if you'd care to use my house with everything in it, you'll find it free and wholly at your disposal. I know just how those things are.

Silversmith. No, madam. Just entertain my wife, that'll do it. Now, what was it you wanted when you were about to look for me?

Cristina. Only to have you weigh this chain and tell me something about its quality and value.

Silversmith. I've examined the chain several times, and I know it's twenty-two-carat gold, worth a hundred and fifty crowns. So if you buy it at that price and don't pay anything more for the workmanship, you won't be cheated.

Cristina. I'll have to add a bit for the workmanship, but not too much.

Silversmith. Madam, be careful how you manage it, because if you ever want to sell the chain, I'll see that you get ten ducats more for the workmanship.

Cristina. If I can help it, it'll come to less. But I hope you're not mistaken about its weight in gold and its quality.

Silversmith. That would be the day if I made mistakes about my own business! I tell you, madam, I've gone over that chain twice, link by link; I've weighed it and know it like my own two hands.

Cristina. Then that's all we need to know.

Silversmith. And to prove it further, I know that the

fellow who came to have it weighed and assayed is a certain local gentleman called Solórzano.

Cristina. Good enough, neighbor. You may go now, and I shall do just what you asked me to. I'll take your wife along and see that she's occupied two hours longer, if necessary. Another hour of fun won't hurt anybody, and don't I know it!

Silversmith. Yes, you catch my drift, you know all about it. And so, madam, good-bye.

Exit Silversmith.

Brígida. This precious gentleman Solórzano (and I'm sure that's his name)—when he comes with the Basque, couldn't we ask him to bring along some rich playmate for me? I wouldn't mind if it turned out to be some big Burgundian who's drunker than an Indian chief.

Cristina. There's no harm in asking. But look, he's back already. He's in such a hurry, and all business. Those ten crowns prick and spur him on.

Enter Solórzano.

Solórzano. Well, Madam Cristina, have you satisfied yourself? Was I right about the chain?

Cristina. Tell me, sir, what is your name?

Solórzano. Don Esteban de Solórzano is what I'm called at home. But why do you ask?

Cristina. To put the final touch of approval on your great honesty and courtesy. Now, sir, you entertain Madam Brígida while I get the ten crowns.

Exit Cristina.

Brígida. Master Solórzano, don't you have any scrap or toothpick left for me? Because, quite frankly, I'm not ready to be thrown in the corner, just like that. I've just as many gentlefolk coming and going to my house as Madam Cristina has. And if I weren't afraid of being overheard, sir, I'd tell you a bit about her many bad points. For instance, her breasts—they're like a pair of empty saddlebags, and her breath's not exactly so sweet either, because of the junk she puts in and on her mouth. And yet, in spite of that, men come flocking, courting and loving her, so that I'm ready to tear at my face, more in anger than in envy, because there's nobody to give me a hand and so many to give me the boot. Well, the ugly ones have all the luck.

Solórzano. Don't despair, madam. If I can help it, your luck will change.

Enter Cristina.

Cristina. Here are the ten crowns, Don Esteban, and there'll be a supper here tonight fit for a prince.

Solórzano. Well, our donkey's waiting at the foot of the street. I'll go bring him. He'll be a hard pill to swallow, but be nice to him, madam.

Exit Solórzano.

Brígida. I told him, dear, to bring someone to cheer me up, and he said he'd do it, all in good time.

Cristina. All in good time, my pet, goes for every one of us. As the years pass there'll be no one to cheer us up. Youth brings great profit—age, great loss.

Brígida. I also told him how very sweet and clean and pretty you are—amber, musk, and civet all wrapped in one.

Cristina. Yes, dear, I know how you praise your friends when their backs are turned.

Brígida (*aside*). Look at her, she gets all the lovers although there's more to the sole of my shoe than to all the frills in her collar. I'll say it again: the ugly ones have all the luck.

Enter Quiñones and Solórzano.

Quiñones. Basque, you grace kiss me hands, you just ask me.

Solórzano. The gentleman from Biscay says he kisses your grace's hands and is at your service.

Brígida. Oh, what a beautiful language! I don't understand it at all, but how beautiful it sounds!

Cristina. I now kiss the gentleman's hands, and more later.

Quiñones. You look good, pretty. Also, we eat together tonight. You keep chain, I no sleep. Enough I give you.

Solórzano. My friend says that you strike him as being good-hearted and handsome, that he wishes supper prepared, that he gives you the chain even if he does not stay overnight, for presenting it to you will satisfy him completely.

Brígida. Did you ever hear of such an Alexander? Luck, luck, we're just swimming in luck!

Solórzano. If you can spare a bit of sweets and a drop of St. Martin's wine for the Basque gentleman, I am sure he'll repay it a hundredfold.

Cristina. Can I spare it, indeed! I'm off to get them; I'll give him more sweets than Prester John of the Indies ever had.

Exit Cristina.

Quiñones. You lady who stayed, as good as left one.

Brígida. What's he saying, Master Solórzano?

Solórzano. That the lady who stayed behind, meaning you, madam, is as good as the one who just left.

Brígida. How right this Biscayan gentleman is! Surely there's nothing of the jackass in him when he says that.

Quiñones. Jackass, the devil. Basque smart as you want.

Brígida. I understand him. He says the devil is the jackass, but the Basques are sharp when they want to be.

Solórzano. Precisely. You hit the nail on the head.

Cristina returns with a servant (either male or female); they are carrying a box of preserves, a decanter of wine, a knife, and some napkins.

Cristina. I'll have the Basque gentleman know he may eat hearty and shouldn't be squeamish; everything in this house is the quintessence of cleanliness.

Quiñones. Wine sweet with me and water you call good. You show him Saint. I drink him this one and other one too.

Brígida. Gracious, how nicely the good gentleman puts it, though I don't understand him at all!

Solórzano. He says that the water or wine is equally good with sweets, but since the wine is St. Martin's, he'll have another drink.

Cristina. As many as he likes, and all that he can take!

Solórzano. Don't give him any more; it's not good for him, as you can readily see. I've told Master Azcaray not to touch a drop of wine, but he won't listen to me.

Quiñones. We go now—wine go up, wine go down, tongue is iron, feet is fetters. I come back evening, lady. Guard you with God.

Solórzano. Just listen to him, and see how right I am!

Cristina. Master Solórzano, what did he say?

Solórzano. That the wine fetters his tongue and binds his feet, that he'll return this evening, and meanwhile, God keep you both from harm.

Brígida. Oh, sinner that I am, look at how cross-eyed and tongue-tied he is! Goodness, there he goes staggering already! How much he must have drunk! It's the saddest thing I've ever seen: so young and such a tippler!

Solórzano. He was already polluted when he left home. Madam Cristina, just prepare the supper while I take him along to sleep off the wine, and we'll be back early this evening.

      Exeunt Solórzano and the Basque.

Cristina. Everything will be ready. Meanwhile, good luck to you both.

Brígida. Cristina, my pet, show me the chain, and let me feast my eyes on it a little. My, how pretty, how new and sparkling it is! And what a bargain! I must say Cristina, willy-nilly you're showered with gifts. Luck just streams through your doors and you don't even lift a finger. Really, you're the luckiest of the lucky. Not that you don't deserve it all; you're so natural, so trim, and so grand, you have the charm to make the most rakish and debonair men fall for you. Not like me, I can't even charm a cat with a handful of crumbs. Take back your chain, dear, or I'll burst into tears—not that I envy you but that I'm sorry for myself.

Solórzano returns.

Solórzano. The worst possible thing has happened to us!

Brígida. Heavens! The worst possible? What is it, Master Solórzano?

Solórzano. As we were turning off your street on our way home we met a servant of the father of our Basque friend. He brought a letter saying that the father is on the point of dying and the son must return home at once if he wishes to see his father still alive. He has enough money for the trip and no doubt must leave at once. I've taken ten crowns from him to give you; here they are, together with the ten you gave me before. Now give me the chain, and if the father survives, the son will be back to return it, or else my name isn't Don Esteban de Solórzano.

Cristina. I'm sorry to hear this, really—and not for selfish reasons, but because of his misfortune. I'd taken a liking to the young man.

Brígida. Ten crowns, without doing a stitch of work —that's wonderful. Take them, dear, and let Master Solórzano have the chain.

Cristina. Here it is; I'll take the money. I was really going to spend over thirty crowns on the supper.

Solórzano. Madam Cristina, you can't cheat an old dog like me. Don't pull the wool over my eyes, I'm not one of your country bumpkins. I'm a horse of a different color.

Cristina. Why all the proverbs, sir?

Solórzano. So you'll understand you can't have your

cake and eat it too. I suppose you thought my promise wasn't worth a tinker's damn. Did you also think you wouldn't have to pay the piper? Well, what's sauce for the goose is sauce for the gander. Madam Cristina, my dear madam, where quick money is concerned, easy come, easy go, you know. Give me back the real chain and keep this fake one of yours. Don't think you can hoodwink me with all your monkey tricks at once. I'll be switched, but they certainly knew how to fake this piece, and quick as a rabbit too!

Cristina. My dear sir, what are you saying? I don't understand.

Solórzano. I say that this is not the chain I gave you, though it's a good imitation. This was made by an alchemist, and the other was genuine twenty-two-carat gold.

Brígida. I declare, that's just what our neighbor the silversmith said.

Cristina. Who the devil could have done this?

Solórzano. Don't bedevil me now. I want my chain back, and no excuses, protests, or curse words, please.

Cristina. Well, the devil take me, though I hope he won't, if this isn't the chain you gave me, and if I ever touched any other. God be my witness if I'm accused of lying about this.

Solórzano. Come, there's no reason to shout. There's a magistrate here who sees to it everyone gets his just deserts.

Cristina. If this reaches the magistrate, I'm done for. He thinks so ill of me he's bound to take the truth of what I say for lies and twist my virtue into vice. Oh, dear sir, if these hands of mine touched any other chain, may cancer consume them!

Enter a Constable.

Constable. What's the trouble here? Who's yelling, who's weeping, who's swearing?

Solórzano. Constable, you've come in the nick of time.

An hour ago, with a certain purpose in mind, I lent this high-tailed Sevillian dame a chain and got ten ducats in exchange. Now when I come back to claim it, she gives me this imitation piece, which isn't worth two ducats, for my genuine twenty-two-carat gold chain worth a hundred and fifty. And wanting to confuse the issue, she sets up a howl, though she knows that this lady, who was here when it all happened, can testify to the truth of what I say.

Brígida. Indeed, I can! I saw it all happen, and twice over! By heaven, so help me God, I must say this gentleman is right, although I can't imagine where the trick was played, because the chain never left this room.

Solórzano. All I ask is that the constable take this lady before the magistrate, for there the truth will out.

Cristina. Again I say: if I am brought before the magistrate, I'm done for.

Brígida. Me too, because I'm not in his good graces either.

Cristina. This time I'll hang myself! This time I'll go mad! This time the bloodsuckers will get me!

Solórzano. Here now, I'll do you a little favor, Madam Cristina, and keep the bloodsuckers away, or at least keep you from hanging. This chain is very like the genuine article that belongs to the Basque. He's so dim-witted and soused he won't know the difference. So I'll bring it to him and tell him it's his. Meanwhile you can grease the constable and pay for tonight's supper. Pull yourself together, the expense won't ruin you.

Cristina. Heaven reward you for this. I'll give the constable six crowns, spend another one on the supper, and from now on, Master Solórzano, I'm your eternal slave.

Brígida. And I'll break my neck dancing for joy!

Constable. Sir, you've behaved like a true, kindhearted gentleman, duty-bound to protect all women.

Solórzano. Give me those ten extra crowns you took.

Cristina. Here they are, and six more for the constable.

Enter two Musicians and Quiñones, the Basque.

Musician. We've heard it all, so here we are.

Quiñones. Now you can really tell Madam Cristina she's been taken, once and for all.

Brígida. Do you all notice how clearly the Basque speaks now?

Quiñones. I never speak unclearly, unless I want to.

Cristina. Oh, believe me, but these rascals have rooked me!

Quiñones. Now, musicians, let's have that ballad I made you learn. How does it go?

Musicians.   *The cleverest woman of all*
        Knows little or nothing at all.

> Although she may boast she knows
> The highest new critical law
> For distinguishing verse from prose,
> Can chat about symbols and myths,
> Quote sources and texts by the score,
> From novels of courtly romance
> To ballads both major and minor
> Of Italy, Spain, or France,
> Or the epical *Don Quixote*,
> Which she rereads every Sunday—
> Though she's learned all this and more,
> She knows little or nothing at all.
>
> Now because she trusts in her wit,
> She will argue by intuition
> Whatever she thinks should fit
> Her premise, then twisting your reason,
> She'll flash you a gloating smile.
> Where the angels, it's commonly known,
> Have feared to tread, she'll trample;
> Where deep still waters run,
> She'll plunge in and raise a squall.
> I'm the cream of all my kind,
> She may think, but knowing so little,
> She really knows nothing at all.

Cristina. Well, then, you've tricked me. But even so, I invite you all to supper tonight.

Quiñones. Oh, it'll all come out in the wash. We accept the invitation.

THE WONDER SHOW

(El Retablo de las Maravillas)

CAST

Chanfalla, manager of the Wonder Show
Little Rebeck (El Rabelín), accompanist
The Governor
Ben Cabbagehead (Benito Repollo), mayor
John Gelding (Juan Castrado), alderman
Peter Sack (Pedro Capacho), notary

Trifles (La Chirinos), manager's wife
Joan Gelding (Juana Castrada), peasant girl
Theresa Cabbagehead (Teresa Repolla), peasant girl
A Dancer, mayor's nephew
A Musician
A Quartermaster
Villagers

The Wonder Show

Enter Chanfalla and Trifles.

Chanfalla. Trifles, don't forget my directions now, especially what I told you about this new trick. It should be as popular as the one we did with the rainmaker drenching the audience.

Trifles. Great Chanfalla, it's stuck in my head like print in a press. Depend on me, I've got a good memory and a good brain, and when they're humming along with the will to please you, they'll top anything else I've got. But tell me, why take on this Little Rebeck? Can't just the two of us manage the job?

Chanfalla. We need him—he's as vital to us as bread. His strumming will cover the gaps while the figures get ready to come on the stage for our Wonder Show.

Trifles. It'll be a wonder if they don't stone us because of that Little Rebeck. Such a godforsaken little midget —in all my born days I've never seen the likes of him!

Enter Little Rebeck.

Little Rebeck. Manager, sir, are you going to put on your show in this town? I'm dying to prove you got a whole and able-bodied worker when you hired me.

Trifles. Four bodies like yours wouldn't add up to half a man. And if your music matches your size, we're done for.

Little Rebeck. Just wait and see. You know, small as I am, I was asked to sign up for a part in a traveling stock company.

Chanfalla. If the part you get equals your size, it will be almost invisible. Trifles, we must be nearing town, and those chaps coming this way are surely the Governor and his aldermen. Let's go greet them. Now sharpen your tongue on the whetstone of flattery, but not too sharply.

Enter the Governor; Ben Cabbagehead, mayor; John Gelding, alderman; and Peter Sack, notary.

My humble greetings to you all, gentlemen. Which one of you is governor of this town?

Governor. I'm the Governor. What do you wish, my good man?

Chanfalla. If I'd an ounce of discernment in me, I'd have guessed at a glance that so ample and peripatetic a figure must belong only to the distinguished governor of this honorable town. If your worship is ever offered the governorship of Algarrobillas, that town of fine hams, refuse it, for you'd put them to shame.

Trifles. And the same goes for your wife and little chaps, if your worship has any.

Sack. The Governor is not married.

Trifles. Whenever he is, then—so my good wishes aren't wasted.

Governor. Very well. Now, my honorable fellow, what is it you wish?

Trifles. May you be long honored, sir, for honoring us this way. Naturally, the oak bears acorns, the pear tree pears, the vineyard grapes, and the honorable man honor, for they can't do otherwise.

Ben. A perfect cicerone sentence, just so.

Sack. Ciceronian. That's what his Honor, Mayor Ben Cabbagehead, meant to say.

Ben. I always mean to say what's right but don't often hit the mark. Well, my fine fellow, what can we do for you?

Chanfalla. Gentlemen, I am Montiel, manager of the

Wonder Show. The Brotherhood of Hospital Charities sent for me from Madrid, where, since there's not a single play manager to be found anywhere, the associated hospitals are going bankrupt. As soon as I arrive, though, everything will be all right again.

Governor. And what do you mean by Wonder Show?

Chanfalla. Because of all the marvelous things it reveals and teaches, it came to be known as the Wonder Show. It was Tomfool the Learned who originally contrived and composed it according to such reckonings, parallaxes, stars, and constellations, modified by such axioms, rhumbs, and Zodiac characters that nobody can see what is going on in the show who is not a pureblood Christian and who was not engendered and procreated in lawful wedlock. So that anyone tainted by these two rather common maladies must abandon all hope of witnessing the marvels, never seen nor heard before, of my Wonder Show.

Ben. Ah, it dawns on me now, there are new things to be seen in the world every day. But what's that? You say the author of this show is called Tomfool the Learned?

Trifles. His name was Tomfool, born in the city of Tomfoolery—a man with a beard, they say, that came way down to his waist.

Ben. Well, generally men with long beards are pretty sharp fellows.

Governor. Alderman John Gelding, with your approval I've decided that Mistress Joan Gelding, your daughter and my godchild, will be married tonight, and to celebrate the occasion I shall ask Master Montiel to produce his show in your house.

John. I am at your service, Excellency, for I approve, subscribe to, and support your decision, whatever stands in the way notwithstanding.

Trifles. What stands in the way is just this: if we're not paid first for our performance, you're not any more likely to see our figures than if you looked from a mountaintop. Now I ask you, your Honors and your Excellencies, is there no soul, no conscience, in your bodies? Where would it leave us if the whole town came flocking tonight to the house of Master John Gelding (or whatever that gentleman is called) and saw the whole show privately, and then tomorrow, when we want to put on a public performance, there wouldn't be a soul in town who hadn't already seen it? No, sir! No, sir, gentlemen! You must pay us a fair price, *ante omnia*.

Ben. Now, Mistress Manager, no Antónia—or, for that matter, no Antony—among us is going to pay you anything. Alderman John Gelding will see to it that you get a good wage, and then some. And if not, the Town Council will see to it. It's clear you don't know us very well. In this town, young woman, we don't expect any of our Antónias to pay for us.

Sack. For pity's sake, Master Ben Cabbagehead, you missed the point! The manager's wife didn't say our Antónias had to pay; what she said was that she wants to be paid in advance, to begin with. That's what *ante omnia* means.

Ben. Look here, Notary Peter Sack, you make them speak straight to me. I don't understand fancy talk. You can read and write, so maybe you understand these Arabian jabberings, but I don't.

John. Good enough. Will the Master Manager be satisfied if I pay six ducats in advance? What's more, we'll take care that none of the townsfolk get into my house tonight.

Chanfalla. I'm satisfied, for I trust your word, sir, as an honorable man.

John. Then come with me. You'll get the money, see my house, and discover how much space there is inside for putting on your show.

Chanfalla. We'll go, but now don't forget the qualifications you need to have if you would dare gaze upon the Wonder Show.

Ben. It's just made for somebody like me. For my part,

tell you I've no reason to be afraid. I'm the son of a mayor with four solid trunks of old Christian stock supporting me on all four sides of my family tree. Don't worry about me seeing that show!

Sack. We expect to see it too, Master Ben Cabbagehead.

John. We weren't born in a ditch, you know, Master Peter Sack.

Governor. Gentlemen—mayor, alderman, notary: so far as I can make out, this will call for all the merit you can draw on.

John. Come, Master Manager, let's get to work. My name's John Gelding, the son of Anthony Gelding and Joan Lusty. I'll say no more to prove and guarantee that I can stand face to face and on my own two feet before the show in question.

Trifles. May God grant it!

> *John Gelding and Chanfalla leave.*

Governor. Mistress Manager, who are the best-favored poets in the capital these days, particularly among the so-called comic writers? For I'm something of a poet myself, a frequenter of the strolling players, a connoisseur of comic masks, cap, and bells. I've written twenty-two plays, all original, one after another. I'm only waiting to be called to the capital and improve the fortunes of half a dozen managers.

Trifles. I don't know what to tell your Excellency about the poets, because there are enough of them to blot out the sun and they all think themselves famous. The comic writers are run of the mill, the most ordinary sort, and so there's no use naming them. But, sir, do tell me, please, what is your Excellency's name?

Governor. My name, Mistress Manager, is Gomezillos the Licentiate.

Trifles. Good gracious! Not that Licentiate Gomezillos who wrote the celebrated songs "Lucifer Took Sick" and "He Fell into a Fit"?

Governor. Some malicious tongues have attributed the lines to me, but I no more wrote them than the Grand Turk himself. What I did write and would not disown concerns the flood in Seville. Although poets steal from one another, I never prided myself on stealing from anyone. As God is my only helper, let others steal if they wish.

Enter Chanfalla.

Chanfalla. You may come in now, gentlemen. Everything is ready. All we have to do is begin.

Trifles. Is the money in the bag?

Chanfalla. Yes, tucked away right here next to my heart.

Trifles. Let me warn you, Chanfalla, the Governor is a poet.

Chanfalla. What do you know, a poet! Well, then, put him down as diddled already, because people of that ilk are a pretty gullible lot—guileless, credulous, and absolutely unworldly.

Ben. Come on, Manager. My feet are ready to hop off by themselves to see those marvels.

They all leave.

Enter the peasant girls Joan Gelding and Theresa Cabbagehead, the former dressed as a bride.

Joan. Sit here, Theresa Cabbagehead my dear, so we'll be right up in front of the show. Now you know about the high qualities one must have to see this show, so be very careful. Otherwise it would be a terrible disgrace.

Theresa. I'm your cousin, you know, Joan Gelding, so enough said about that. I only wish I were as sure of going to Heaven as I am of seeing every bit of this show. Otherwise, if I were so unlucky as to be found wanting—I swear by my mother, may she rest in peace, I'd scratch these eyes out of my head. And I can't see myself doing that!

Joan. Don't upset yourself, cousin; they're all coming in now.

Enter the Governor, Ben Cabbagehead, John Gelding,

Peter Sack, the Manager, his wife, the Musician, some townsfolk, and Ben's nephew, who will be the gentleman dancer.

Chanfalla. Be seated, everyone. The show will take place when this curtain is opened. The manager's wife will come behind it and the musician here will stay in front.

Ben. You call that a musician? Put him behind the curtain too. If I don't have to see him, I'll be glad not to hear him.

Chanfalla. Mayor Cabbagehead, you are wrong to condemn the musician. Indeed, sir, he is a very fine Christian and a well bred hidalgo besides.

Governor. Qualities so essential in a first-rate musician!

Ben. Well-bred? Possibly. Well-tuned? Never!

Little Rebeck. Serves me right for coming here to play before . . .

Ben. By God, we've had musicians here who were just as . . .

Governor. Just stop the argument there with Rebeck's "before" and the mayor's "just as." Otherwise, there'll be no end to this. Master Montiel, you may begin.

Ben. That manager's brought mighty little stuff here to put on such a grand show.

John. I guess that's all part of the mystery.

Chanfalla. Your attention, ladies and gentlemen, the show is about to begin! O thou, whomsoever thou wert who wrought this show with such wondrous skill that it gained renown as the famous Wonder Show, now, by virtue of what it contains, I conjure, command, and compel thee this instant to reveal a few of thy marvelous wonders for this audience's pleasure and delight, yet without creating the least scandal whatever. Ah, now I see thou hast hearkened to my plea, for yonder the great and mighty figure of Samson rises; he embraces the columns of the temple and is hurling it to the ground in vengeance against his enemies. But hold, worthy knight! Hold, by the grace of Almighty God, lest thou committest the offense of crippling and flattening into pancakes so many noble gentlefolk as are now assembled here!

Ben. Stop it, for pity's sake alive! A fine thing for us that would be—coming here for a bit of fun only to end up being ground to dust. Stop it, Sir Samson! Damn those sins of mine, I've always meant to be good!

Sack. Gelding, do you see him?

John. Of course I see him! You think I don't have eyes?

Governor (*aside*). There's something mysterious going on here. I can no more see this Samson than I can the Grand Turk, though I take it I was born legitimate and a true Christian.

Trifles. Man, look out! Here comes the same bull that killed the worker lately in Salamanca! Man, get down! Lie down! God help you! God save you!

Chanfalla. Everybody, down! Down, everybody! Whoa, there! Huish, hish!

> *Everyone throws himself down in a panic.*

Ben. The devil got into that bull. Why, his flanks were all yellow and red. If I hadn't got down, he'd have scooped me right up.

John. Master Manager, if you could, I wish you'd keep those horrible figures away from us. And I don't mean it for myself, but for these girls here. That ferocious bull has left them looking pale as ghosts.

Joan. I should say so, Father! I won't be myself again for days and days. I could see myself stuck on his horns —why, they were sharp as awls.

John. You wouldn't be my daughter if you missed seeing that.

Governor (*aside*). This is too much. They all see something I don't see. Still, to save face, I'll have to say I saw it.

Trifles. That pack of mice scurrying over there are di-

rect descendants of the mice Noah raised on his ark.
Some are white, some are striped, some are speckled, and
some blue, but each and every one of them's a mouse.

Joan. Mice! Help! Save me! Hold me or I'll jump out of
that window! Mercy, Theresa, pull your skirts down or
they'll bite you. On my granny's soul, I swear, few as
they are, they might as well be thousands.

Theresa. Worse luck, I'm the one they're after. They're
swarming all over me. A little brown one's bit me on the
knee. Heaven save me, for there's no one here who can.

Ben. It's lucky I have my long knee breeches on. No
mouse can get in, tiny though he is.

Chanfalla. That shower gushing down so fast now from
the clouds comes from the very spring that flowed into
the River Jordan. Any woman whose face it touches will
find her skin is tanned like burnished silver, and any
man it touches will find his beard turned golden.

Joan. Did you hear that, Theresa? Show your face,
you'll see it will do you some good. Oh, how sweet this
liquor is! Put your hat on, Father; don't get wet.

John. We've got our hats on, daughter, all of us.

Ben. The water's trickling on my back, clear down to
my gutter spout.

Sack. I'm dry as a stick.

Governor (aside). What the devil is this? They're all
drowning and I don't even feel a drop of water. Can I be
the only bastard here, and all the rest legitimate?

Ben. Haul that musician out of here! Otherwise, I swear
to God, I'm leaving and not looking at another figure. The
devil take you—you're no musician but a spook; you sit
there strumming without a zither and no sound out of
you!

Little Rebeck. Now, Mayor, don't get angry with me. So
help me, I'm playing this just as God has taught me to.

Ben. So God's taught you to play! Why, you little

weasel, get right behind that curtain or I'll throw this bench at you!

Little Rebeck. The deuce only knows why I came here.

Sack. How fresh are Jordan's holy waters! Though I covered myself tight as I could, still some of it hit my mustache. Now I'll bet it's turned it as yellow as a bar of gold.

Ben. And a lot worse than it was before.

Trifles. There go at least two dozen lions and honey-eating bears. They're on a rampage! Take cover, everybody. They may be imaginary, but someone's likely to get hurt, if not struck down. They're strong as Hercules, with claws ripping into you like swords.

John. Here, for God sake, Manager, what are you doing now, filling up the house with bears and lions?

Ben. Look, that Tomfool brings us lions and dragons like they were nightingales and larks. Say, Manager, either you show us gentler figures or we stop watching this moment. And then, God help you, because you'll get your walking papers right out of this town.

Joan. Master Ben Cabbagehead—for our sakes, do let the bears and lions come in. We'll be very grateful.

John. What's this, daughter? First you're scared of mice, then you want bears and lions?

Joan. It's just the novelty of the thing, Father dear.

Trifles. This maiden now appearing before you, so trim and elegant, is the famous Herodias, who was once rewarded for her dancing with the head of John the Baptist. If anyone would care to be her partner, you'll see something truly marvelous.

Ben. She certainly is a dazzler, by God! What a juicy little figure! And look at the wench wriggle and swivel! Nephew Cabbagehead, you know how to tickle the castanets, get up there with her and dance, and we'll have a regular revel!

Nephew. I'd like that, Uncle Ben Cabbagehead.

The tune of a saraband is struck up.

Sack. By my grandpa's beard, so they had the saraband and chaconne way back then!

Ben. That's it, Nephew, hold the tricky Jewess tight. But say, if she's a Jewess, how come she can see these marvels?

Chanfalla. There's an exception to every rule, Mayor.

The sound of a bugle or cornet offstage, and an army. Quartermaster comes in.

Quartermaster. Who's the governor here?

Governor. I am. What do you wish, sir?

Quartermaster. Make up billets for thirty armed soldiers, at once. They're due here in half an hour or maybe sooner. There's the bugle call already. So, good-bye.

(Exit.)

Ben. I'll bet that Tomfool wise man sent them.

Chanfalla. Not at all. It's that cavalry company bivouacked two leagues from here.

Ben. Oh, I'm on to that Tomfool of yours, and I know you and he are the world's greatest rascals, not to mention this musician here. So I order you to tell Tomfool that if he dares send those soldiers here, he'll get two hundred lashes on his back, one after another, from me personally.

Chanfalla. I tell you, Master Mayor, Tomfool didn't send them.

Ben. And I tell you he did—just as sure as he sent those other lousy figures I've been looking at.

Sack. We all saw them too, Master Ben Cabbagehead.

Ben. I don't deny it, Master Peter Sack. Stop that strumming, you half-finished dream of a musician, or I'll break your head!

The Quartermaster returns.

Quartermaster. Hey, what's this? Aren't the billets ready? We've got the horses in town already.

Ben. What? Is that Tomfool still up to his old tricks? I tell you now, you manager of smoke and shadows, you're going to pay for all this!

Chanfalla. You're all witnesses now: the Mayor threatened me.

Trifles. You're all witnesses now: the Mayor referred to the orders of his Majesty the King as the orders of Tomfool.

Ben. Woman, may the good God Almighty tomfool you before my very eyes!

Governor. In my opinion, these are real soldiers and not a hoax.

Quartermaster. What do you mean, a hoax? Have you lost your mind, Governor?

John. They could easily be tomfooleries, like all the other things we've been watching here. Come on, Manager, bring out that Herodias girl again, and let this gentleman see what he's never seen before. Maybe then we can bribe him to get right out of town.

Chanfalla. Right you are! And now see how she returns, motioning her partner to join her again.

Nephew. I'm game. By all means.

Ben. That's the way, Nephew. Wear her down, wear her out! Whirl her round and around. God, what a wench! She's shaking like quicksilver! That's it, that's it! Go to it, give it to her!

Quartermaster. Why, they're all balmy! What the devil kind of girl do they mean? Where's the dance, and what's this Tomfool?

Sack. Oh? So the Quartermaster doesn't see the Herodias girl?

Quartermaster. What the hell sort of girl should I see?

Sack. That's enough: *he's one of them.*

Governor. *He's one of them, one of them.*

John. The Quartermaster is one of them. *He's one of them,* he sure is one of them.

Quartermaster. I'll be a son of a bitch like the rest of you! Great God alive, once I draw this sword, you'll all go flying out that window, and I don't mean the door either.

Sack. It's clear: *he's one of them.*

Ben. Yes, it's clear: *he's one of them.* He just doesn't see a thing.

Quartermaster. Filthy rabble, say that again and I'll break your bones, each and every one of you!

Ben. Your heretics and bastards are always cowards, and that's why we just have to say, over and over: *he's one of them, he's one of them.*

Quartermaster. All right, you stinking peasants—you asked for it!

He draws his sword and slashes away at them; the Mayor beats up Little Rebeck; and Trifles pulls down the curtain, saying:

Trifles. The Devil blew that bugle and brought those soldiers in the nick of time—just as though we'd rung a bell to call them.

Chanfalla. We've had wonderful good luck. The point of the show's been proved, and tomorrow we can put it on before the townsfolk. Meanwhile, we've won this round, so congratulations are in order: Three cheers for Trifles and Chanfalla!

THE CAVE
OF
SALAMANCA

(La Cueva de Salamanca)

CAST

Pancracio

Student, Carraolano

Sacristan, Reponce

Barber, Nicholas

Leoniso, friend of
Pancracio

Leonarda, wife of
Pancracio

Cristina, housemaid

The Cave of Salamanca

Enter Pancracio, Leonarda and Cristina.

Pancracio. Mistress, dry those tears and stop your sighing. Remember, I'll be away four days, not centuries. On the fifth day, at the latest, I'll be back, God preserve me. But if it upsets you so, just say the word and I'll break my promise and give up the trip altogether. Surely my sister can get married there without me.

Leonarda. Pancracio, dear lord and master, I don't want you to be discourteous because of me. Go now, God speed you, and meet your obligation, since the matter is so pressing. My grief I'll keep to myself and spend the lonely hours as best I can. Only, I beg you to come back and not stay any longer than you promised. Oh, help me, Cristina, I've a pain in my heart!

Leonarda faints.

Cristina. Ah, weddings and holidays—such dreadful things! Indeed, sir, if I were you, I'd never go there.

Pancracio. Run inside, girl, and get me a glass of water to throw in her face. No, wait, I know a few magic words I'll whisper in her ear; they can revive people who faint.

He speaks the words and Leonarda recovers, saying:

Leonarda. Enough. It can't be helped. I must be patient. My dear, the more you linger, the longer you delay my happiness. Your friend Leoniso should be waiting for you in the carriage. God be with you and bring you back as quickly and safely as I could wish.

Pancracio. If you want me to stay, my angel, I'll be like a statue and not budge an inch.

Leonarda. No, no, sweet comfort. Your wish is my desire, which means you must leave and not stay here, for your honor and mine are one and the same.

Cristina. Oh, mirror of matrimony! If all wives cherished their husbands as my mistress loves hers, they'd sing a different tune.

Leonarda. Go get my shawl, Cristina. I must see your master safely off in his carriage.

Pancracio. No, I beg you. Kiss me, but stay here, please. Cristina, be sure and cheer up your mistress, and I'll get you a pair of shoes when I return.

Cristina. On your way, sir, and don't you worry about my mistress. I'll see to it we both enjoy ourselves so she won't miss your absence.

Leonarda. Enjoy myself? Me? What a fantastic idea! Without my love beside me, I can know no bliss or joy, only grief and sorrow.

Pancracio. I cannot bear this any longer. Ah, light of my eyes, farewell; I'll see nothing to delight me till I gaze upon you once again.

Exit Pancracio.

Leonarda. Good-bye, and good riddance to you! Go, and don't come back! Vanish, go up like smoke in thin air! Good God, this time all your bluster and squeamishness don't move me a bit!

Cristina. And I was afraid your sweet nothings would keep him here and spoil our fun.

Leonarda. Do you think our guests will really come tonight?

Cristina. And why not? I've been in touch with them, and they're just dying to come. This afternoon they had the washerwoman, our confidante, bring a hamper that's full of gifts and goodies, disguised as laundry. It's like one of those huge baskets the King distributes to his beggars on Maundy Thursday, except this one's an Easter basket with pies, cold meats, blancmange, and two capons that haven't even been plucked yet, together with all sorts of fresh fruits too. And last but not least, a huge, four-gallon skin of wine that smells absolutely divine!

Leonarda. That's my Reponce, generous as ever, my sweet sacristan, the darling of my heart.

Cristina. And what about my Nicholas? He's the barber of my heart, the razor that whisks away my troubles, so that when I'm with him it's as though I never had a care in the world.

Leonarda. Did you put the hamper away safely?

Cristina. It's in the kitchen, covered by a straining cloth to hide it.

The Student, Carraolano, knocks at the door and then walks right in.

Leonarda. Cristina, see who it is.

Student. Ladies, it's me, a poor student.

Cristina. It's quite clear you're poor and a student— first by the rags you wear, and second by your nerve. The idea that every beggar nowadays can't wait for alms in the doorway but must march right into a house and sniff around in the corners without caring if he wakes anybody up or not!

Student. I expected a gentler reply from one so gracious as yourself—especially since I neither wished nor expected anything more than a loft and a bit of straw to wrap myself in tonight against the inclemencies of Heaven, which, as far as I can observe, now seem to threaten earth with the greatest severities.

Leonarda. And where do you hail from, my friend?

Student. I am a Salamantine, my lady. That is, I am a native of Salamanca. I was on the way to Rome with an uncle, who died on the road in the heart of France. Then, being alone, I decided to return home. But I was robbed in Catalonia by the lackeys or henchmen of Roque Guinarde, who was not himself present at the time. Had he been there, he would never have permitted me to be so insulted, for he is most courteous and gracious, and generous besides. Night overtook me at these sacred portals, as I regard them, and now I throw myself upon your mercy.

Leonarda. Really, Cristina, this student moves me. I pity him.

Cristina. He tears my heart to pieces. Let's keep him here tonight—surely the peasantry can live on the castle's leftovers; I mean, his hunger will find enough relics to prey on in what's left of the food. And besides, he can help me pluck the poultry in the basket.

Leonarda. What's this, Cristina, are we going to fill the house with witnesses to our little revel?

Cristina. He looks like the sort of fellow who'd rather stay mum than go hungry. Come here, friend. Do you know anything about plucking?

Student. Do I know anything about plucking? I don't know what you mean unless you want to make fun of me because I was stripped of my money. But there's no need for that, since I readily admit it: I'm the most cleanly plucked person alive.

Cristina. I didn't mean that; I was only asking if you could pluck a few capons.

Student. What I'd like to say to that is that I am, my dear ladies, by the grace of God, a bachelor of arts from Salamanca, and I can't say——

Leonarda. Of course in that case you can pluck not only capons but also geese and wild turkeys. Now, how good are you at keeping a secret? Or are you the sort who itches to tell all he sees, thinks, or feels?

Student. You could kill more men right in front of me than sheep in a slaughterhouse and I'd never breathe a word.

Cristina. Well, see to it that you keep your mouth shut tight, stitch up both ends of your tongue with a latchet, sharpen your teeth, and join us. You'll see mysteries and dine on marvels, and then you can measure your length for a cozy sleep in the straw.

Student. Seven feet is all I need; I'm not in the least greedy or particular.

Enter Sacristan Reponce and the Barber.

Sacristan. Hail, ye Achillean charioteers, helmsmen of our pleasures, light beams in our darkness, ye two reciprocating loves who, as pedestals and pillars, serve the amorous manufactory of our desires!

Leonarda. That's the one thing wrong with him. Reponce dear, please speak plainly, so that I can understand, and don't go flying up so high I can't follow you.

Barber. That's where I come in. I speak plainer than the sole of your shoe. I can call a spade a club or a club a spade—or whatever it is.

Sacristan. Yes, and there ought to be a difference between a sacristan who knows Latin and a plain barber who knows one tune.

Cristina. As for me and what I want of him, my barber knows as much Latin as Erasmus, if not more. But let's not talk about learning or learn about talking now; everyone speaks as he can, if not as he should. So let's go in and get to work; there's lots to do yet.

Student. And lots to pluck.

Sacristan. Who is this fine fellow?

Leonarda. A poor Salamancan student who begged to be put up overnight.

Sacristan. I'll give him something for bed and supper, and let him be on his way.

Student. My dear Sacristan Reponce: I cheerfully accept your charity, thank you. But though I'm sworn to silence and a plucking job to oblige the young lady who invited me here, I'm no dumbwaiter, and I'll be damned if I leave this house tonight, no matter who says so! Blast you, can't you trust a man of my ability who's willing to sleep in a hayloft? And if you're so touchy about your capons, get the Devil to pluck them for you and gobble them up yourself till you burst a gut!

Barber. This fellow sounds more like a rogue than a beggar. He looks like someone who'd rob you blind and walk away.

Cristina. I'll be robbed and plundered, but I like his spirit. Now let's go in and get things organized while our beggar boy plucks away, silent as a church mouse at Mass.

Student. At vespers, more likely.

Sacristan. That miserable student scares me; I'll bet he knows more Latin than I do.

Leonarda. That's just where he gets his spirit—from knowing so much Latin. But don't regret your charity to him, my dear; remember, charity "is the greatest of all things."

Exeunt omnes.

Enter Pancracio and his friend Leoniso.

Friend. I knew that wheel was about to collapse, but there's no one so stubborn as a coachman. If he'd just taken a short detour around the ditch, we'd have been two leagues on our way by now.

Pancracio. I'm not worried a bit. I'd rather go back and spend the night with my wife, Leonarda, than stay at the inn. When I left her this afternoon, she was more dead than alive at my going.

Friend. A wonderful woman! Heaven's been good to you, my friend. You should be grateful.

Pancracio. I'm as grateful as can be, but that's still not enough. Why, there's no Lucretia as chaste, no Portia as wise as she is. She is virtue and devotion rolled into one.

Friend. If my wife weren't so jealous, I'd have no complaints. My house is closer down this street; go that way, my friend, and you'll be home quickly. So, till tomorrow, when I find us another carriage, good-bye!

Pancracio. Good-bye!

Exeunt Pancracio and Friend.

The Sacristan and the Barber enter with their guitars; Leonarda, Cristina, and the Student. Enter the Sacristan, with his cassock pulled up and tied around his waist, dancing to the music of his own guitar, and with every caper he shouts these words:

Sacristan. Marvelous night, marvelous time, marvelous supper, marvelous love!

Cristina. Dear Sacristan Reponce, now's not the time for dancing. Eating our supper comes first, and then the other things; so leave off dancing till the time comes.

Sacristan. Wonderful night, wonderful time, wonderful supper, wonderful love!

Leonarda. Let him be, Cristina. I love to watch his nimble feet.

Pancracio knocks at the door.

Pancracio. Are you asleep in there? Don't you hear me? What's this? You've bolted the door so early? Oh, my Leonarda, she's so terribly cautious.

Leonarda. Ah, worse luck! I know that voice and that knock. It's my husband, Pancracio. Something must have happened to bring him back. Go hide in the coal bin—I mean in the garret, where we keep the charcoal. Run, Cristina, and show them where. Meanwhile, I'll put him off and give you time to get away.

Student. Horrible night, terrible time, impossible supper, miserable love!

Cristina. Stormy weather ahead, no doubt of it. Come on, all of you!

Pancracio. What in the world is this? Here, here, open up, sleepyheads!

Student. That settles it. I'm not getting involved with those fellows. Let them hide where they like—show me the way to the hayloft, and if I'm found there, at least I'll be taken for a beggar, not an adulterer.

Cristina. Hurry, before he batters the house down!

Sacristan.   My heart's in my mouth.

Barber.   And mine's in my shoes.

> *Exeunt omnes, except Leonarda,*
> *who peers through the window.*

Leonarda.   Who's out there? Who's knocking?

Pancracio.   It's your husband, Leonarda dear. Open up, I've been pounding at this door for half an hour.

Leonarda.   Your voice does sound like my darling Pancracio's. But one cock crows like another, so I can't be sure.

Pancracio.   Ah, the caution, the amazing honesty of that woman! My dear, it's me, your husband, Pancracio. Don't be afraid, it's quite safe to open the door for me.

Leonarda.   Come closer, and I'll see about that. What was it I did when Pancracio left this afternoon?

Pancracio.   You sighed, you wept, and then you fainted.

Leonarda.   That's right. But tell me now: What are the marks I have on one of my shoulders?

Pancracio.   On your left shoulder there's a birthmark the size of a small coin; it's got three hairs on it like fine gold threads.

Leonarda.   That's right. But now tell me, what's the maid's name here?

Pancracio.   Come on, pet, don't be tiresome. Her name is Cristina. Anything else?

Leonarda.   Cristina, Cristina! It's your master! Let him in, dear girl.

Cristina.   I'm coming, madam. He'll be ever so welcome! What's wrong, dear master? What brings you home so soon?

Leonarda.   Oh, my darling! I am afraid something terrible has happened. Tell us quickly or I shall faint.

Pancracio.   It was only that the coach cracked a wheel in the ditch, so my friend and I decided to come home instead of spending the night out. Tomorrow we'll find some way to go—there's plenty of time. But what's all that shouting?

Offstage, and as though far off, the Student shouts:

Student. Open up, somebody, I'm suffocating!

Pancracio. Is that in the house or out on the street?

Cristina. I'll be tied if it isn't that poor student I locked in the hayloft for the night.

Pancracio. A student in my house while I was away? Hm, sounds bad! Now, madam, if I weren't so sure of your good character, I'd begin to suspect something's behind this locking-up business. But go, Cristina, and let him out. All that hay must have tumbled down on him.

Cristina. I'm going.

Leonarda. Dear, it's just a poor Salamancan boy who begged us in God's name for a night's lodging, even if it were only in the hayloft. And you know how I am, unable to refuse anybody anything when I'm asked. So we shut him in. But here he comes, and you can see for yourself.

Enter the Student and Cristina; his clothes, his head, and his beard are all covered with straw.

Student. If I were bolder and had fewer scruples, I could have avoided the risk of suffocating in straw; I'd have dined better and had a softer and safer bed.

Pancracio. Who, my friend, would have given you a better supper and a better bed?

Student. Who? Why, my own ingenuity—if fear of the law hadn't tied my hands.

Pancracio. A dangerous sort of ingenuity, if it makes you fear the law!

Student. If I could only use the science I learned in the Cave of Salamanca (my native town) without fear of the Holy Inquisition, I'd be able to eat and stuff myself, regardless of expense. And yet, perhaps I might use the science this once, when necessity compels and excuses me, though I don't know if the ladies can keep a secret as well as I did.

Pancracio.　Never mind about them, my friend. Do what you want, and I'll see to it they keep quiet. I must certainly see something of the things they say are taught in the Cave of Salamanca.

Student.　Would you like me now to conjure up two demons in human form carrying in a hamper full of cold meats and delicacies?

Pancracio.　Demons in this house, before my very eyes?

Leonarda (aside).　Gracious me! Heaven preserve me from the likes of them, or else I'm lost!

Cristina (aside).　The very devil's got into that student! Pray God be kind to us now. My poor heart's pounding in my throat!

Pancracio.　Well, now, if it can be done safely and not frighten anybody, I'd enjoy seeing those gentlemen demons and the hamper full of cold meats; but I warn you again, the demons mustn't scare us.

Student.　I say they shall appear in the shapes of the sacristan of this parish and of his friend the barber.

Cristina.　You don't mean Sacristan Reponce and Master Nicholas, our own barber? Poor fellows, to find themselves turned into devils! But tell me, brother, will they be baptized devils?

Student.　What a notion! Where the devil would you find baptized devils, and why would devils be baptized anyway? But maybe these are baptized, for there's no rule without an exception. Now stand back; you're about to see wonders.

Leonarda (aside).　The jig's up! Here's where it all comes out! Here's where our sins walk out in the open! Here's where I die of shame.

Cristina (aside).　Courage, madam. A stout heart overcomes any misfortune.

Student. Hear me, you miserable creatures, come out
Of that coal bin, you're in disgrace.
Be quick, and make sure you've the grace
To bring that hamper of cold meats out.
Don't try to provoke me, I can conjure less
Gently; don't dally, I say. Come out!
Because if you don't, I've no case
And my magical purpose falls on its face.

All right, then. I know just how to treat these half-
human little devils. I'll go in there myself and cast such
a powerful spell over them that they'll come flying out—
though by the looks of the poor devils, they'll take plain
coaxing better than spellbinding.

Exit the Student.

Pancracio. I tell you, if it all turns out as this fellow
says, it will be the most astonishing thing on earth.

Leonarda. Of course he'll do it, why not? How can he
possibly deceive us?

Cristina. There's a commotion inside. I'll bet he flushes
them out. See how he drives those demons, and look at
that wraith of a hamper they're carrying!

Enter the Student, the Sacristan, and the Barber.

Leonarda. Good Lord! See how much they resemble
Sacristan Reponce and the town barber!

Cristina. Madam, take care. You mustn't say the Lord's
name in front of demons.

Sacristan. Say whatever you wish; we're like the black-
smith's dogs, who fall asleep to the banging hammer:
nothing frightens or upsets us.

Leonarda. Bring them closer so I can eat out of their
hamper—and you eat too.

Student. I'll try it first, and begin with the wine.
(*Drinks.*) An excellent wine—and from Esquivias, Mr.
Sacri—demon?

Sacristan. It *is* from Esquivias, I swear to——

Student. Hold on there, blast you! Don't you dare say another word! I know all about you blasphemous demons! Little demon, little demon, we haven't come here to commit mortal sin, but to while away an hour or so, chatting and eating, and then be on our way.

Cristina. And these fellows, must they eat with us?

Pancracio. Surely demons don't eat.

Barber. Some do and some don't, but we're some who do.

Cristina. Oh, Master, oh, Mistress! Do let the poor devils join us, since it was they who brought the supper. It wouldn't be polite to let them go off dying of hunger. Besides, they seem to be such decent, well-behaved little devils.

Leonarda. If they're not going to frighten us, and if my husband is willing, they're entirely welcome.

Pancracio. Let them stay. I'd like to see a thing or two that I never saw before.

Barber. Pray God repay you for your generosity, good people.

Cristina. Oh, how well-bred, how courteous they are! I'll be robbed and plundered, but if all devils are like these, then devils are my friends from now on.

Sacristan. Now everybody listen to this, then you'll really fall in love with us.

The Sacristan plays and sings, and the Barber joins him only in the last line of each stanza.

Sacristan.   Hear me, you who know so little,
        And I'll tell you somewhat more
        Of the knowledge that's essential

Barber.   *In the Cave of Salamanca.*

Sacristan.   First listen to what's been inscribed
        By that college man Two-Tanker
        On his mare's or filly's hide,
        But more especially upon
        The backside such a creature raises.

On this, of course, he sang the praises

Barber.   *Of the Cave of Salamanca.*

Sacristan.   There you know that side by side
The beggar studies with the banker,
And the narrower the mind
On starting, the broader it departs.
Professors sitting down to lecture
Find they're stuck to pitch and tar.
One expects such lively starts

Barber.   *In the Cave of Salamanca.*

Sacristan.   Occidental Moors get lessons
In discretion at this college
Where one hears the dumbest students
Burst with scientific knowledge.
Once a man gets in, with rank or
Not, nothing more can faze him; so
Hip-hip-hurray, and hi-di-ho,

Barber.   *Dear old Cave of Salamanca.*

Sacristan.   And if our student conjurer
Hails from grapevine country, let
All his vineyards grow and prosper
With luscious grapes both red and white.
Any devil with the rancor
To deny this will be cudgeled
And externally expelled

Barber.   *From the Cave of Salamanca.*

Cristina.   Enough. Must devils be poets too?

Barber.   Just as sure as all poets are devils.

Pancracio.   Tell me, my good man, since you devils know everything, where did they start all those dances we call the Saraband, the Sambapalo, the I'm-So-Sorry Fling, and now this Escarramán, the latest thing?

Barber.   Where? In Hell, of course—wholly and solely in Hell.

Pancracio.   Yes, that's what I think.

Leonarda.   But really, though I'm quite fond of it, I

don't dare do the Escarramán—people would call me a hussy!

Sacristan. Ah, but if I taught you a few new steps every day, you'd be a first-rate dancer in a week. In fact, I can tell you—you're quite good at it already.

Student. All that can wait. First let's go in and dine; that's the important thing now.

Pancracio. Yes, let's go in. I want to find out if devils eat or not, and a hundred thousand other things I've heard said about them. And, for pity's sake, don't leave my house till you've taught me all the arts and sciences you've learned in the Cave of Salamanca.

THE
JEALOUS
OLD HUSBAND

(El Viejo Celoso)

CAST

Strawtubes (Cañizares),
   old man

His Friend

Mistress Lorenza, Straw-
   tubes' wife

Cristina, her niece

Nettlesome (Hortigosa), a
   neighbor

A Gallant, who is silent

A Constable

A Dancer

Musicians

The Jealous Old Husband

Enter Mistress Lorenza, her maid Cristina, and her neighbor Nettlesome.

Lorenza. It's just a miracle he didn't lock me in, Mistress Nettlesome. Oh, my wretched yoke and my despair! This is the first time since I married him that I've spoken to anyone from outside the house. If I could only push him out of my life—him and the priest who married us!

Nettlesome. Come, come, Mistress Lorenza, don't take on so. When the old pot's worn out, you buy a new one.

Lorenza. Proverbs and old wives' tales! That's just the sort of thing that roped me in. The devil take all his money (but not the coins with crosses on them). The devil take all his jewels and fine gifts; the devil take everything he's given me or promised me. What good's any of it to me if I'm still poor with all that wealth, starving in the midst of plenty?

Cristina. Dear Aunt, you've good reason to say so. I'd rather go around with a rag in front and another in back and have a young man than be stuck in the mud with that smelly old creature you took for a husband.

Lorenza. I took him, Niece? My word, they forced him on me. Being so young, I was all obedience. If I had had the slightest notion of these things, I'd have sooner bitten my tongue off with these teeth than have said "Yes" to him—the three-letter word it takes three thousand bitter years to unsay. But I suppose it was fated to be.

When something's fated that way, there's nothing a poor human being can do to stop it.

Cristina. Gracious, and such a mean old man! All night long—"Cristina, bring me the pot. Here, Cristina, take it away. Get up, bring me some hot towels; my back's killing me. Here, give me the straw tube, my kidney stone's worn me out." He's got more ointments and medicines on his table than a drug store, and me—with no time to see if I'm even dressed—having to run around nursing him. Phew, phew, that decrepit old thing! All ruptured and jealous—and there's just no one more jealous on earth.

Lorenza. It's the God's honest truth—every word she says.

Cristina. I wish I didn't have to say it.

Nettlesome. Well then, Mistress Lorenza, just do what I tell you and see how wonderful everything turns out. This young man's one in a million—a fine lover, knows how to keep his mouth shut, and really appreciates a favor. So now, since the old man's so jealous and watchful, and there's no time to exchange sweet nothings, screw up your courage, be bold, and follow the plan we worked out. I'll bring the fellow to your room, then take him away, and all done so smoothly the old man won't see a thing, even if he had a hundred eyes or could see deeper than a water dowser, who they say can see ten yards down through solid earth.

Lorenza. I never tried this before, and I'm bashful. I wouldn't risk my reputation just to have a little fling.

Cristina. Dear Aunt, you remind me of that old ditty about Gómez Arias:

> Oh, Mister Gómez Arias,
> It's your pity I implore;
> So shy and innocent a lass,
> I never sank so low before.

Lorenza. The things you won't say, Niece! Surely some evil spirit makes you say them.

Cristina. I don't know about that, but I do know I'd do everything Mistress Nettlesome says, barring nothing.

Lorenza. What about my honor, Niece?

Cristina. What about enjoying ourselves, Aunt?

Lorenza. And what if we're found out?

Cristina. And what if we're not?

Lorenza. And what's to assure us we won't be?

Nettlesome. What else but caution, cunning, and wit? But most of all, a bold front and my strategy.

Cristina. Look, Mistress Nettlesome, bring the young man here. See to it he's gallant and neat, easygoing and a bit dashing, but most of all, young.

Nettlesome. The man I promise you has all these qualities plus two more: he's rich and generous.

Lorenza. I can do without riches, Mistress Nettlesome. I'm swamped in jewelry, and the sheer variety of my wardrobe makes me dizzy. As far as that goes, I couldn't ask for anything more, thanks to poor Strawtubes, God bless him. He's bought me more clothes than a fashion show and more trinkets than a jewelry shop. If only he didn't nail down my windows, bolt my doors, snoop around the house day and night, and throw out all the dogs and tomcats simply because they're male. If he'd stop putting such queer restrictions on me, I'd gladly forgo the gifts and favors.

Nettlesome. What, is he such a jealous fool?

Lorenza. Let me tell you. The other day he had a chance to buy a good tapestry at a real bargain, but since it had full-sized human figures, he turned it down and bought another tapestry with a simple landscape on it, something not as good and more expensive. Besides the street door, there are seven doors leading to my bedroom, and each of them is under lock and key. But where he keeps those keys at night, I'll never know.

Cristina. Oh, Aunt, I'm sure he tucks the master key away inside his nightshirt.

Lorenza.   Don't you believe it, Niece. Don't I sleep with him? I've never seen or felt a key on him.

Cristina.   Worse than that: he stalks through the house all night like a boogeyman. And if there's any music in the street, he throws stones down at the musicians to drive them away. He's just a mean, wicked, little wizard, and an old man—and there's nothing worse I can say.

Lorenza.   Mistress Nettlesome, you'd better go now. If the old crank finds you here, we might as well forget about the whole thing. Do what you have to, but quickly. I'm so sick of this, I could tie a rope around my neck and end this dreary life of mine.

Nettlesome.   Once you consider the new life in store for you now, you'll forget such morbid ideas and start having brighter and more cheerful ones.

Cristina.   I'd give a finger off my hand to see that happen. It kills me to see the aunt I love so much wasting away, caught in the clutches of that dotty old—and doubly old—dotard. I just can't stop calling him old.

Lorenza.   But really, Cristina, he's quite fond of you.

Cristina.   That doesn't keep him from being a dotard, does it? Besides, I've heard that old men always have a hankering for young girls.

Nettlesome.   You're quite right, Cristina. Good-bye for now. I'll be back after supper. And, madam, you just think of our little plan, then see how smoothly we manage all the ins and outs of it.

Cristina.   Mistress Nettlesome, do bring me a cute little friar to play with.

Nettlesome.   Girl, I'll bring you one—and sweet as a picture.

Cristina.   I don't want a picture friar. I want a live one, a live one—tiny and precious, like a pearl.

Lorenza.   And if your uncle sees him, what then?

Cristina.   I'll say it's a goblin, and that'll scare him, and then I'll have my fun.

Nettlesome. I'll be sure to bring you one. But now, good-bye.

Exit Nettlesome.

Cristina. Look here, Aunt. If Nettlesome brings the gallant and my little friar too, and if the master happens to see them, all we have to do is grab him, all of us together, and choke him dead and drown him in the well or bury him in the stable.

Lorenza. Knowing you, I think you'd just as soon do it as say so.

Cristina. Well, why doesn't he stop being such a jealous old man and let us alone? We don't do him any harm, and we go on living here like saints.

Exeunt.

Enter the old man, Strawtubes, and a Friend of his.

Strawtubes. My friend, my dear friend: a seventy-year-old man who marries a girl of fifteen is either out of his mind or yearns to get to kingdom come in a hurry. I married this little Lorenza because I wanted some company, a little comfort, someone at my bedside to close my eyes when I come to die. I no sooner got married than I ran into a tornado of troubles and heartaches. I had a house till marriage unhoused me. My lodgings were peaceful till marriage dislodged me.

Friend. That was a bad mistake, my friend, but not a fatal one, for as Paul the Apostle says, "It's better to marry than to burn."

Strawtubes. There was nothing burnable in me, my friend. The slightest spark would reduce me to ashes. I wanted a companion, so I looked for a companion, and I found a companion. Now God help me—for there's no one else who can.

Friend. Are you jealous, my friend?

Strawtubes. Of the sun glancing at her, of the breeze touching her, of her own skirts rubbing against her.

Friend. Has she given you reason to be jealous?

Strawtubes. Positively not! There's no way she possibly

could, and no ifs or buts about that! Besides being locked
with a key, the windows are shuttered and have iron bars.
No door is ever opened. No neighbor dares cross my
threshold, and while I'm alive no one ever will. Remember this, my friend: women don't pick up bad habits by
going to fairs, parades, or public gatherings, no matter
how many. Where they're spoiled, where they slip, and
where they really tumble is at a friend's or a neighbor's house. A nasty woman like that packs more wicked-
ness inside her than darkest midnight. And more assignations are made and brought off in her house than in
any crowd outside.

Friend. I can believe it. But if Mistress Lorenza never
leaves the house and if nobody ever gets in to see her,
why are you so continually worried?

Strawtubes. Because some day little Lorenza will find
out what she's been missing and that'll be terrible—so
terrible that just thinking about it frightens me; and fright
drives me to despair, and my despair galls me continually.

Friend. You've good reason to be frightened, because a
woman wants all the enjoyments of matrimony straight-
forward.

Strawtubes. My wife enjoys them doubled—I mean,
twice . . . over.

Friend. Maybe that's just what's wrong, brother.

Strawtubes. No, no, absolutely not. Lorenza's innocent
as a dove, and so far she doesn't know a thing about
such complicated ideas. And now, good-bye, my friend.
I'm going home.

Friend. I'd like to go along and meet your wife, Mistress Lorenza.

Strawtubes. Friend, you know that old Roman proverb
that goes: *Amicus usque ad aras,* meaning, "A friend as
far as the altar." That's to say, friends should do everything for each other except what goes against their
Maker. Now, my friend, I say *usque ad portam,* as far
as the doorway, meaning that no one oversteps the

threshold of my patience. And so good day to you, my friend, and pardon me.

Exit Strawtubes.

Friend. I've never in all my life seen anyone so suspicious, so jealous, or so obnoxious. He's one of those fellows who go dragging a rope to his own hanging—the kind that die of the sickness they dread.

Exit the Friend.

Enter Mistress Lorenza and Cristina.

Cristina. Uncle is a long time coming, Aunt—but Mistress Nettlesome is even longer.

Lorenza. I hope he never gets here, and Nettlesome too. He makes me mad and she rattles me.

Cristina. Oh, Aunt, the fun's all in taking a chance, and if it doesn't turn out all right, forget it.

Lorenza. Good gracious, Niece! If I know anything about such things, it's that all the trouble starts with taking a chance.

Cristina. Aunt dear, really. Where's your courage? If I were your age, a gang of bandits wouldn't frighten me.

Lorenza. I say it again, and I'll go on saying it: Satan himself puts the words in your mouth. But what's that now? How did he let himself in?

Cristina. He must have used the master key.

Lorenza. The devil take him and his master keys!

Enter Strawtubes.

Strawtubes. Who's that you were speaking to, Mistress Lorenza?

Lorenza. I was speaking to Cristina.

Strawtubes. Consider it carefully now, Mistress Lorenza.

Lorenza. I say I was speaking to Cristina. Who else would I be talking to? You think, by any chance, it might be someone else?

Strawtubes. I wouldn't want you to be soliloquizing about anything that would reflect unfavorably on me.

Lorenza. I don't understand you and your circumlo-quizing, and I don't even care to. Let's give ourselves a holiday and stop fighting.

Strawtubes. I wouldn't fight with you, holiday or not. But who's that banging on the door now? Go see who's there, Cristina. If it's a beggar, give him something and get rid of him.

Cristina. Who is it?

Nettlesome. Mistress Cristina, it's Nettlesome, your neighbor.

Strawtubes. Nettlesome—and a neighbor? Heaven help me! Cristina, ask her what she wants and give it to her, as long as she doesn't step over the threshold.

Cristina. And what is it you want, neighbor?

Strawtubes. The word "neighbor" gives me the willies. Call her by her right name, Cristina.

Cristina. Just tell me—what is it you want, Mistress Nettlesome?

Nettlesome. I have something urgent to ask of Master Strawtubes. It involves my honor, my life, and my very soul.

Strawtubes. Niece, tell that woman I'd forfeit all those things myself, and more, just to keep her out of this house.

Lorenza. Gracious, how strangely you carry on! Aren't I standing right here with you? Is someone going to devour me with his eyes? Or carry me off in thin air?

Strawtubes. Well, let her in with all her buzzing demons, since that's what you want.

Cristina. Come in, neighbor.

Strawtubes. Neighbor—oh, that fatal word!

Enter Nettlesome, carrying an embossed sheepskin wall hanging, in the four corners of which are

*painted the figures of the famous knights Rodamonte,
Mandricardo, Ruggiero, and Gradasso. Rodamonte
appears muffled in a cape.*

Nettlesome. Kindest sir: hearing of the wide renown
that your good name enjoys, your reputation for great
charity and philanthropy, I plucked up the courage to
come beg you to show me such great good mercy, charity,
and generosity as to purchase this wall hanging, because
I have a son in jail for the injuries he inflicted on a cloth
shearer, and the magistrate is keeping my son imprisoned
until the surgeon makes his deposition, and I have no
money to bribe him, and my son now runs the risk of
being fined even more, which might easily come to a great
sum because he is very mischievous, and I want to get
him released today or tomorrow, if possible. The workmanship is good, the material is brand new, and yet I'll
let you have it, sir, for whatever it's worth to you, because there's more involved here than money, and I'm
used to sacrificing in such ways all my life. My dear lady,
take hold of this end and let us spread it open so that
Master Strawtubes can see for himself that I'm not trying to cheat him. Raise it a bit, dear lady. Now, see how
full and long it is; see how each painting seems to leap
out, as if it were alive.

*When the hanging is held up and raised full length, a
Gallant slips out into a room behind. Inspecting
the paintings, Strawtubes remarks:*

Strawtubes. My, that's a handsome likeness of Rodamonte! But what can this muffled little gentleman want
in my house? If he knew what I thought of such tricked-
out figures, he'd jump out of his wits.

Cristina. Uncle dear, I know nothing about muffled
gentlemen, and if one's got into the house, it's Mistress
Nettlesome's fault. Believe me, and may the devil take
me if I had anything to do with his getting inside. No, I
swear, it would be the very devil if my uncle blamed me
for this.

Strawtubes. Yes, Niece, I can readily see it's Mistress
Nettlesome's fault—which doesn't surprise me, because

how should she know how I feel or how much I hate such figures in a tapestry?

Lorenza. He's just talking about painted figures, Cristina—that's all.

Cristina. Of course, that's exactly what I'm talking about. (*Aside to Lorenza.*) God help me! Now I'm all right again, but for a moment my heart was in my shoes.

Lorenza (*aside to Cristina*). There you were, sounding off like a woodpecker. It serves me right, to be sharing secrets with a child!

Cristina (*aside*). Oh me, oh my! That was close! I almost let the cat out of the bag.

Strawtubes. Mistress Nettlesome, I'm not fond of muffled figures nor of any muffling at all. Here, take this doubloon; that should take you out of your difficulty. And now, take yourself out of my house as fast as you can go, and I mean right now—and take that hanging with you.

Nettlesome. Long life to you, sir—live longer than Methuselah in Jerusalem, for the sake of Mistress—whose name I don't know but whom I'd gladly serve night and day with all my heart and all my soul, and I know her soul's as pure as a little turtledove's.

Strawtubes. Mistress Nettlesome, abridge your leave-taking and go. And stop meddling with other people's souls.

Nettlesome. If my good lady needs any sticking plasters for female troubles, I have some marvelous ones; or if she has a toothache, I know some magic words that'll stop the pain—like that!

Strawtubes. Enough, Mistress Nettlesome. My wife has no female troubles and no toothaches. All her teeth are good and sound and she's never had one pulled yet.

Nettlesome. But Heaven knows, one day they'll go bad, because she has a long life ahead of her, and with old age all teeth go to rack and ruin.

Strawtubes. In God's name, won't I ever get rid of this

neighbor! Nettlesome, devil, neighbor, or whatever you are—get out of this house and leave me alone!

Nettlesome. That's fair enough, so don't get angry, sir, I'm going now.

Exit Nettlesome.

Strawtubes. Oh, neighbors, neighbors! All those fine words of hers burn me up, and just because they come out of her neighborly mouth.

Lorenza. I say, what a barbarian, what a perfect savage you are! What in the world did this neighbor say to make you so dead set against her? All your good deeds are done in mortal sin. So you gave her twenty-four gold pieces, but along with that went your twenty-four insults, your wolfish fangs, your scorpion's bite, and your malicious tongue.

Strawtubes. No, no. It was an ill wind blew in that pile of unthreshed corn. And I say it's a bad sign when you're so hot to defend your neighbor.

Cristina. Please, Aunt, won't you go to your room and rest, and leave Uncle to himself? He's just losing his temper.

Lorenza. Yes, Niece, that's what I'll do. And mark me, he won't see hide nor hair of me for the next two hours. I'll make him take his medicine, even if he gags on it.

Exit Mistress Lorenza.

Cristina. Uncle, did you hear how she slammed that door? Now I'm sure she's looking for a crossbar to keep it bolted.

Lorenza (*within*). Cristina? Cristina dear?

Cristina. Yes, Aunt, what is it?

Lorenza. If you could only see the handsome young man fate has sent me! So young—so tall, dark, and handsome! Oh, his breath is sweet as orange blossoms.

Cristina. Gracious, how silly, how childish! Aunt, are you mad?

Lorenza. Not in the least; I've got all my wits about me.

I tell you, if you saw him, your heart would sing with joy.

Cristina.   Gracious, how silly, how childish! Scold her, scold her, Uncle; don't let her say such shameless things, even as a joke.

Strawtubes.   Lorenza, have you lost your mind? I'm in no mood for your little pranks.

Lorenza.   It's no prank, it's the simple truth—I mean the biggest truth of its kind there ever was.

Cristina.   Gracious, how silly, how childish! Aunt, just tell me this: is my little friar there too?

Lorenza.   Not now—but, Niece, he'll come yet, as neighbor Nettlesome promised.

Strawtubes.   Lorenza, say anything you like, but don't dare use that word "neighbor" again; it makes me shiver all over to hear it.

Lorenza.   I'm shivering too, but with love, thanks to my neighbor.

Cristina.   Gracious, how silly, how childish!

Lorenza.   Now I begin to see what you are, you miserable old man—how you cheated me all these years.

Cristina.   Scold her, Uncle—scold her, Uncle! She's being utterly shameless!

Lorenza.   Oh, let me bathe this young man's angelic little beard in a basin of rose water. His face is so sweet, like a painted angel's.

Cristina.   Gracious, how silly, how childish! Tear her apart, Uncle!

Strawtubes.   Not her, but the door she's hiding behind is what I'll tear apart.

Lorenza.   There's no need to. I open it freely. Come in and see for yourself that everything I said is true.

Strawtubes.   Though I know you're joking, I'll come in, just to calm you down.

As Strawtubes steps inside the door a basin of water

is hurled in his eyes; he turns aside to dry himself.
Cristina and Lorenza busy themselves over him
while the Gallant appears and slips out.

Strawtubes. By God, Lorenza, you almost blinded me! The devil with your eye-splashing little jokes.

Lorenza. Just look what I'm stuck with for a husband —the most suspicious man on earth! Look how quick he is to believe my fibs just because he's so—so sunk to the ears in jealousy that he must grind me down and ruin my happiness. Should I tear out my hair for what this old man can't give me? Should I cry my eyes out because of this sinful old wretch? See how lightly he treats my honor and good name when he turns suspicions into facts, lies into truth, takes my jests seriously, and spits his curse on my little game. Oh, this tears the heart out of me!

Cristina. Aunt, don't shout so much! You'll bring all the neighbors running.

Constable (*within*). Open the door! Open it at once or I'll knock it down.

Lorenza. Go open it, Cristina dear. Let the world learn about my innocence and this old man's cruelty.

Strawtubes. I swear it, Lorenza, I really thought you were joking! Keep quiet, Lorenza!

Enter the Constable, Musicians, a Dancer,
and Nettlesome.

Constable. What's all this? What are you quarreling about? Who's shouting here?

Strawtubes. It's nothing at all, sir—just the usual spat between husband and wife. It soon blows over.

Musician. Good God! My friends and I here, we're musicians, and we were playing at an engagement party next door when we heard the shouting and that stopped us dead; so we came rushing over, thinking something awful was going on.

Nettlesome. And so did I, with my guilty conscience.

Strawtubes. Yes, that's true, Mistress Nettlesome; if it hadn't been for you, nothing of the sort would have happened.

Nettlesome. So now I'm blamed for it! It seems I've got the kind of luck that always makes me get blamed, willy-nilly, for everyone else's sins.

Strawtubes. Gentlemen, if you'd all please go now, you have my best wishes and thanks for your kind intentions. My wife and I have patched things up.

Lorenza. Yes, I'll accept that, but first you'll have to beg my good neighbor's pardon for thinking so ill of her.

Strawtubes. If I'm to be forgiven by all the neighbors I've thought ill of, there'll be no end to it. Anyhow, I do beg your pardon, Mistress Nettlesome.

Nettlesome. Oh, you're forgiven, henceforth and retroactively.

Musician. Well, we can't let it go as a false alarm. Strike up a tune, friend. Dancer, go to it. And we'll celebrate the reconciliation with a song.

Strawtubes. Gentlemen, I can't stand music. I'll pay you though, and consider it played.

Musician. Like it or not, here goes.

They sing.

The rain that falls on St. John's Day
Pollutes the wine and ruins bread.

But quarrels fought on St. John's Day
Ensure a peaceful year, it's said.

The Dancer dances.

When rain beats down on drying wheat
And the tender blooming vine,
There is no farmer who can keep
His produce safe or store his wine.

Quarrels fought on St. John's Day

(The kind that make you curse and weep)
Ensure a peaceful year, they say.

The Dancer dances.

On dog days, when the sun is hot,
Tempers flare up on the spot.
Once those days are past and gone,
Angers wane and cheeks turn wan.

So what's been said is not a lie:
Have your quarrel on St. John,
Then watch a year of peace roll by.

The Dancer dances.

Spats between a wife and hubby,
May they always end this way:
From cat-and-dog to lovey-dovey,
All forgiven, smiled away.
The same holds true for any sun
That's wriggled through a cloud: it's happy.

Have your quarrel on St. John,
Then watch a year of peace roll by.

Strawtubes. Now you can all see the stresses and strains I've been under because of this neighbor. So judge for yourselves if I shouldn't distrust each and every one of her kind.

Lorenza. Though my husband distrusts neighbors, I could kiss you dear neighbors, one and all.

Cristina. So could I. But if my neighbor had brought me a sweet little friar, I'd have thought her a much better neighbor. And so, dear neighbors, good-bye.

SELECTED BIBLIOGRAPHY

Other Works by Cervantes

La Galatea, 1585   Pastoral romance
Don Quixote, Part I, 1605   Novel
Novelas Exemplares, 1613   (Signet CT 157)
Viaje del Parnaso, 1614   Burlesque poem
Don Quixote, Part II, 1615   Novel
Persiles y Sigismunda, 1617   Novel

Selected Biography and Criticism

Arbó, Sebastián Juan. *Cervantes: The Man and His Time.* New York: The Vanguard Press, 1955.

Bell, Aubrey F. G. *Cervantes.* Norman, Okla.: University of Oklahoma Press, 1947.

Benardete, Mercedes J., and Flores, Angel (eds.). *Cervantes Across the Centuries.* New York: The Dryden Press, Inc., 1947.

Busoni, Rafaello. *The Man Who Was Don Quixote.* New York: Prentice-Hall, Inc., 1958.

Entwistle, William J. *Cervantes.* London: Oxford University Press, 1940.

Fitzmaurice-Kelly, James. *Cervantes and Shakespeare.* London: Humphrey Milford, 1916.

Fitzmaurice-Kelly, James. *Cervantes in England.* London: Oxford University Press, 1905.

Frank, Bruno. *A Man Called Cervantes.* New York: The Viking Press, Inc., 1935.

Krutch, Joseph W. *Five Masters: A Study in the Mutations of the Novel.* Bloomington, Ind.: Indiana University Press, 1959 (paper).

Madariaga, Salvador de. *Don Quixote*. London: Oxford University Press, 1935.

Schevill, Rudolph. *Cervantes*. New York: Duffield & Company, 1919.

Tomás, Mariano. *The Life and Misadventures of Miguel de Cervantes*. Boston: Houghton Mifflin Company, 1934; London: George Allen & Unwin, Ltd., 1934.

Unamuno, Miguel de. *The Life of Don Quixote and Sancho According to Miguel de Cervantes Saavedra*. Trans. by Homer P. Earle. New York: Alfred A. Knopf, 1927.